A Mountain Bi

C000029866

to the
Highways & Bridleways
of
DORSET

Steve Wrann

1st edition published August 1993
Reprinted October 1995

ISBN 1-898073-02-3

© Power Publications
1 Clayford Ave.,
Ferndown, Dorset

Acknowledgments

I would like to thank my wife Lesley for her patience and support and for her help in reading the original scripts and maps. Andy Galpin for his tireless assistance with the computer, all the kind souls who tested the routes and my family, colleagues and friends for their encouragement and support.

All rights reserved.

No part of this publication may be reproduced, stored in a retrieval system, or transmitted in any form or by any means (electronic, mechanical, photocopying, recording or otherwise) without the prior permission of the copyright holder.

Publisher's Note

Whilst every care has been taken to ensure the accuracy of all the information given in this book neither the author nor the publisher can accept responsibility for any mistakes that may occur.

Other Publications available:

A Mountain Bike Guide to the Highways and Bridleways of The New Forest and Hampshire

STD PHONE NUMBERS

Please note all phone numbers in the area covered by this publication now need the figure 1 inserted after the initial zero.
For example: (0202) (the code for Bournemouth) becomes (01202).

Printed by Pardy & Son (Printers) Ltd, Ringwood, Hampshire.

Front cover illustration by David Horwood.

Introduction

I thought I would introduce this book by highlighting a few of the thoughts behind the project. Firstly why write a mountain bike guide for Dorset? I was inspired by the superb book The Highways and Byways of Dorset by Sir Frederick Treves (first published in 1906) and the ever increasing number of walking guides of the area to get out and really explore my native county. Without doubt at the moment there is a gap in the plethora of literature available on the region, there are no books aimed at those with bikes as their mode of transport rather than shank's pony. I therefore decided that whilst I was getting lost in the Dorset hinterland I should endeavour to write a guide encouraging others to do the same. I also felt it may provide me with an opportunity to publish a few of my jokes but very few people apart from myself seem to laugh at them so only a few have sadly (I think it's sad) escaped the humour watchdog's editing knife.

The county has no mountains or even really big hills to speak of but it does have a vast labyrinth of bridleways and infrequently used quiet country roads. The county is unusual in that there are no motorways devouring the pastoral landscape and apart from the ever expanding conurbation in the east and the busy tourist routes Dorset is peaceful, rural and largely unspoilt by the ravages of modern society. It is an ideal place to escape the rat race.

My aim has been to produce a visually attractive book with simple maps linked to an easy to follow route description. The routes are not designed to appeal to the mindless few who go screaming through the countryside whooping and hollering and generally giving mountain biking a bad name but to those who wish to enjoy the countryside for what it has to offer. I have tried to link places of interest that you would not normally see when travelling through the country by car and strongly recommend that you take the time to explore these and the surrounding areas. The routes vary in length and difficulty and are written to tempt as many cyclists as possible from the hardened mud loving mtbeer to the youngster with a new bike wishing to explore the countryside and everyone in between. There are certain parts of the area where there are not many bridleways and to ensure that the routes cover most of the county and it's very diverse landscapes some of the routes are entirely on tarmac and can therefore be ridden on almost any sort of bike, however, most require a true mountain bike.

For a good many of the routes you will need to use a car to get to the starting location, in most cases there is a public car park fairly close by but for those where there is not please park with consideration for others.

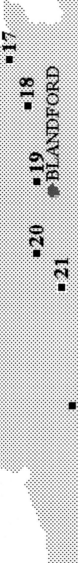

GILLINGHAM ■15

SHAFTESBURY ■16

■17

■18
BLANDFORD

■19
■BLANDFORD

WIMBORNE

■20

28,29&30 ■

■31

BOURNEMOUTH

■21

■24

■25

POOLE

■1
■2
SWANAGE

■3

■26
WAREHAM

■4

■22

■23

5&6 ■

SHERBORNE ◆ ■14

12&13 ■

■7
DORCHESTER

WEYMOUTH

■8

BEAMINSTER ◆ ■11

■9

BRIDPORT
■10

Contents

Each route is set out in the same easy to follow format with the following sections.

ROUTE TITLE: the name and number of each route plus the total mileage. The number before the oblique stroke indicates the total distance and the second figure the off-road total (if any).

START LOCATION AND ACCESS: a brief description of where the route begins (including the OS grid reference) and how to get there including the nearest railway station if appropriate (see next page).

WARNINGS AND HIGHLIGHTS: as one rider's highlight is another one's fear this section provides a short list of possible areas of excitement or hazards.

PUBLIC HOUSES: a selection of pubs that are on the route but outside of the main towns. A list of telephone numbers is included in case you wish to check whether food is available or on the opening times.

PLACES OF INTEREST: a list of places or things of interest on or near the route including telephone numbers where appropriate. If you intend to visit a particular place please check on their opening times to avoid disappointment. At the end of each section there is a short list of additional things to look out for during the ride.

LINK INFORMATION: a brief description on how routes within the same area can be connected together in order to make a longer ride.

ROUTE INFORMATION: the total distance is indicated next to the route heading and the off-road distance is shown after the oblique stroke. Details regarding the grade of the ride are shown on the relevant route map. I have not included, as is common with ride guides, an estimate of the time required to cycle the route. I believe everyone has a different reason for cycling and it therefore follows that times will vary accordingly.

ROUTE NARRATIVE: I have tried to make each narrative as easy to read and follow as possible. The language is very simple and to the point as I personally do not think flowery prose is appropriate in such a guide and also am not that good at it! I have also avoided the peculiar, although often very amusing, language of the mountain bike magazines. The route is broken down into small numbered sections linked to the map, in most cases this will mean (I hope) that it is not necessary to refer to an OS map, however I strongly recommend that you do in time purchase the appropriate ones as they will provide an invaluable reference point for further exploration. That said it is very likely that you will get lost on one route or another and a map will be useful but when you are loudly cursing me remember that getting lost is all part of the fun.

When bridleway signs indicate the destination of the trail I refer to this in the description, where the route is only way marked, e.g. with a blue arrow I have called these "Marked Bridleways" and not surprisingly the remainder are known as "Unmarked". The County Council are gradually updating the signs on the bridleway network although there are still areas where the signs are few and far between the position is improving all the time. All the routes have been checked against the definitive rights of way maps at the central library and any queries checked with the County Council. On the whole I have used bridleways that are ridable although it may be necessary to push the bike in places and the route warnings generally indicate where.

When I have used the word 'towards' it generally means that you do not reach the place mentioned but only head in its direction. That may sound as though I am teaching your grandmother to suck eggs but then I can't imagine she is out cycling with you.

RAILWAYS: many of the routes start near or are easily accessed from railway stations however, there are a few problems with the service provided for cyclists and the main restrictions are during the peak commuter travel times, in practice this will probably only affect those wishing to travel from London. The main line running from Waterloo through Southampton to Weymouth generally has sufficient space to carry several bikes and these are carried free of charge. This is a very good service, sadly the remaining lines through Dorset, i.e. from Weymouth northwards and through Sherborne and Gillingham are appalling, there is very limited space (unbelievably one bike per train) and it is necessary to book in advance! British Rail publishes several leaflets and it is certainly best to obtain copies of these if you intend to use the network or contact your local station for up to date information.

SIX OF THE BEST: throughout the book are some brief lists of various highlights.

The Off-Road Code

♦ Only ride where you know it is legally OK to do so. Since the late sixty's cyclists have had permission to ride on public bridleways, these are marked by a blue arrow. Cyclists may also ride on roads used as public paths (RUPP'S) and byways open to all traffic (BOATS) which are sign posted with a red arrow. You must NEVER cycle upon a public footpath which incidentally are marked by a yellow arrow. Do not cycle on private land without the permission of the owner.

♦ Remember all off road rights of way are classified as highways and therefore the Highway Code applies.

♦ Always be courteous and take care not to offend anyone you may meet. Always yield to horses and pedestrians, if you need to pass them slow to walking pace and warn of your approach.

♦ Where possible stick to the main trail in order to avoid unnecessary erosion and damage to the surrounding environment, if this means cycling through a puddle, do so.

♦ Avoid livestock wherever possible. If the bridleway passes through an occupied field take care not to scare animals.

♦ Never leave any litter.

♦ Do not make any unnecessary noise.

♦ When riding in groups avoid bunching that will cause a hazard to other users.

♦ Fasten all gates.

♦ Never create any kind of fire hazard.

THE FORESTRY COMMISSION: I have been advised by the Commission that they operate an open access policy for cyclists in the forests of Dorset subject to a few restrictions.

♦ Do not cycle on way marked walks.
♦ Do not cycle on tracks that are less than two metres wide.
♦ Do not cycle into the planted areas of trees or across areas recently cleared.
♦ Do not cycle across areas of heather or land under repair.
♦ Do cycle with consideration for other forest users and at moderate speeds.

It is my understanding that in due course they will be producing an appropriate leaflet giving more details of their overall policy.

Safety Precautions

♦ Always wear an approved helmet! Most helmets indicate whether they have passed the rigorous tests of ANSI and SNELL and these are the words to look for.

♦ Wear appropriate clothing and footwear - dress in layers so that you may easily make adjustments for changes in temperatures and where possible in clothes designed for mountain biking or active outdoor pursuits. Check the weather forecasts before venturing out and prepare for the worst.

♦ Carry some form of identification.

♦ Inform someone where you are going and what time you expect to return. Carry sufficient coins in case it becomes necessary to make a telephone call. Allow plenty of time to complete a ride within daylight hours. The routes within this guide are such that an average of 6 mph should be achievable without undue stress.

♦ Never over stretch yourself and try to rest for about 5 minutes every hour.

♦ Before starting any ride ensure that your bike is safe to ride. At the very least check the following:- brakes and cables, the wheels and tyres and the chain and gear mechanisms.

♦ Carry a small first aid kit and try to have a rudimentary understanding of first aid.

♦ Carry some emergency food rations and plenty of liquid. Avoid excessive alcohol at any pub stop, not just because of the effect upon your senses but also because of its diuretic effect.

♦ Always cycle under control and avoid skidding. Do not cycle so fast that it is not possible to stop safely within the clear distance ahead of you. Be aware of other vehicles using tracks especially farm and forestry access roads.

♦ Carry a small tool kit including the following:- puncture repair kit, spare inner tube, pump, tyre levers, multi-purpose tool or the more cumbersome collection of allen keys, adjustable spanner and chain splitter.

♦ It is preferable to carry a compass and an Ordnance Survey map but I hope the route descriptions within this guide will be sufficient.

♦ Take time to admire the scenery whilst your are stationary.

Please remember that I am not an expert and all the above information has been gleaned from a collection of sources and my own experience.

Route Information

On each map there is an indication of north and a scale above which there is a combination of circles and triangles, these are a guide of the difficulty of each ride and an explanation follows.

GRADE OF RIDE

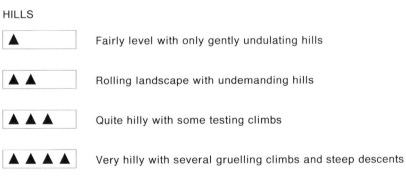

●	Suitable for beginners - country roads and gravel tracks
● ●	Fairly easy going - mostly well drained tracks and grassy lanes
● ● ●	Testing conditions in places
● ● ● ●	Technically demanding and tricky in places

HILLS

▲	Fairly level with only gently undulating hills
▲ ▲	Rolling landscape with undemanding hills
▲ ▲ ▲	Quite hilly with some testing climbs
▲ ▲ ▲ ▲	Very hilly with several gruelling climbs and steep descents

OFF-ROAD EXTRA
This indicates an area where there are bridleways or forest tracks you may wish to explore to add further enjoyment to your ride.

Map Key

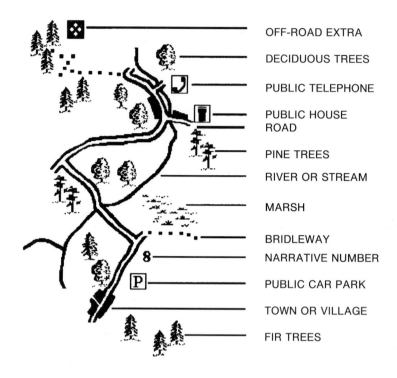

OFF-ROAD EXTRA

DECIDUOUS TREES

PUBLIC TELEPHONE

PUBLIC HOUSE
ROAD

PINE TREES

RIVER OR STREAM

MARSH

BRIDLEWAY

NARRATIVE NUMBER

PUBLIC CAR PARK

TOWN OR VILLAGE

FIR TREES

Public telephones, car parks and pubs are shown on the maps where possible in their location however, this is not always possible especially in the towns and villages where the symbol merely indicates that the facility is available.

All towns and villages are indicated with capital letters. Places of interest, rivers, landmarks etc. are written in italics. It must be noted however, that not all the places of interest are open to the public and some can only be viewed from the road or bridleway.

Although I have tried to make the maps fairly accurate you must make allowance for a certain amount of artistic licence and the fact that they are not all printed to the same scale.

The Isle of Purbeck

The very varied geological structure of the region is a microcosm of the United Kingdom and ranges from the exposed chalk cliff tops to the peaceful clay valley and broad heath lands. The obvious natural attractions have made the area very popular with many different sections of society appealing to the sun worshippers, hikers, horse riders, rock climbers, sailors, twitchers, holidaymakers and mountain bikers alike unfortunately, the irresponsible behaviour of a few means that mountain bikers get a bad press. It is therefore all riders responsibility to behave in a sensible unselfish manner so that we may all enjoy this beautiful area in a harmonious future. This may sound a little pious but it is true and the restrictions imposed in the New Forest are evidence of what could happen. That said the Isle of Purbeck is a mountain bikers paradise there are numerous bridleways and quiet winding roads over very diverse terrain. However, this can mean at weekends some popular areas become crowded and I strongly recommend cycling during 'off peak' periods such as during the week or on a Saturday morning. The following routes offer a taster of the many different opportunities and should form a good basis on which to explore the Purbeck Isle. All four rides can easily be linked as they all have a part of one or the other, if that's not double Dutch, on the route and a brief study of the maps and text will reveal this. In order to avoid duplication on each route description I have listed the following information in one place.

NEAREST RAILWAY STATIONS: Wareham from the west or Poole or Parkstone if accessing the Isle via the ferry. In the future the Swanage steam railway may link up with Wareham and as well as being a tourist attraction it may be an added bonus to the infrastructure of the area.

PLACES OF INTEREST

Corfe Castle: The National Trust owned castle (0929 480921) dominates the village there are however, other attractions including a small museum, the model village, an interesting church, several charming shops and of course the ale houses.

Studland: A small village with an interesting Norman church. It is very quiet apart from the tramp of hikers boots during the weekends and the babble of the sun worshippers during the summer months.

Wareham: Popular historic market town whose attractions include the Saxon Walls, a small museum, the very interesting St Martin's church and the Quay as well having more than it's fair share of pubs.

Worth Matravers: This attractive stone village with a pretty pond is a superb starting point for a bracing WALK along the beautiful rugged southern coastline or a ride to St Aldhelm's Head and it's curious church and marvellous views.

The area has many other attractions and these include the RSPB reserve at Arne, Blue Pool (0929 551408), Church Knowle animal sanctuary (0929 480474), and the traditional seaside resort of Swanage.

PUBS

Church Knowle	The New Inn	0929 48035
Corfe Castle	The Greyhound	0929 480205
	The Fox	0929 480449
	The Castle Inn	0929 480208
	The Bankes Arms	0929 480206
Kingston	The Scott Arms	0929 480270
Studland	The Bankes Arms	0929 44225
Worth Matravers	The Square and Compass	0929 439229

1. Studland Heath

8/5 miles

START LOCATION AND ACCESS: Studland is well sign posted throughout the whole of the Purbeck Isle and is easily reached from Swanage, Corfe Castle and the Sandbanks Ferry. The Bankes Arms is well sign posted in the village.
OS MAP REF.: 036827

WARNINGS AND HIGHLIGHTS

- Very popular area for ramblers - take the utmost care not to offend people in this sensitive patch
- Stiff climb to Ballard Down
- Very exposed along the clifftops
- Tricky conditions across the heathlands - rocky, sandy and boggy areas all presenting different challenges.

Look out for the beautiful natural meadow near Old Harry in the early summer, the beaches, and the large glacial deposit on the heathlands - Agglestone Rock.

[1] From the Bankes Arms cycle down the hill, at the bottom just beyond the public toilets turn left up the slight incline along the rough track. Follow the well-worn and very popular track to Old Harry.

[2] The bridleway runs almost parallel to the cliff edge follow it straight ahead. Ignore the option to veer right through the small isolated gate, turn right at the end of the meadow on the clearly more popular route up the hill.

[3] Progress past the triangulation pillar to the Obelisk, once there veer right down the steep hill to the road. Turn right up the hill and then left at the junction towards Corfe Castle.

[4] Opposite the small golf course there is lay-by on the right side of the road. Pass through the gate onto the stony bridleway, cycle across the main golf course with care and consideration for the golfers. Initially follow the bridleway towards Rempstone but then turn towards Greenland, the narrow track is rough and in places technically demanding whilst in other places it is so sandy it is almost impossible to cycle. Cross the very marshy area via the gravel 'bridge' and then follow the narrow trail towards Rempstone. After you have passed through the large field continue straight on ignoring the route to Rempstone, pass through several gates and then on past the barns to a chalky track, follow this straight ahead and then round to the right towards the road.

[5] At the road turn right and head back to Studland; once in the village follow the signs back to the Bankes Arms.

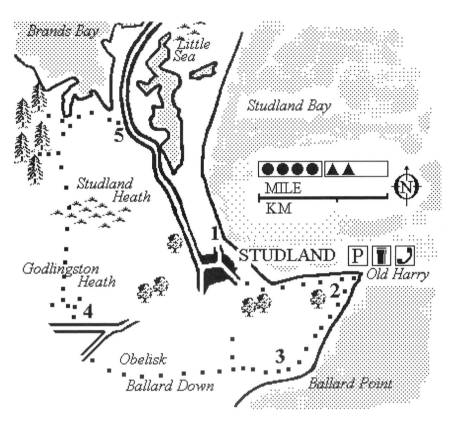

Brands Bay

Little Sea

Studland Bay

5

Studland Heath

MILE

KM

N

STUDLAND

Old Harry

P

1

2

Godlingston Heath

4

Obelisk

Ballard Down

3

Ballard Point

Old Harry Rocks

2. South Purbeck Hills   18/10 miles

START LOCATION AND ACCESS: Ulwell lies on the road between Studland and Swanage. There are two lay-bys near the small water works opposite the caravan park.
OS MAP REF.: 021809

WARNINGS AND HIGHLIGHTS
♦ In places the route is very exposed to the elements
♦ Fast descent towards Kimmeridge and further on towards Corfe Castle
♦ Very testing climb to Ridgeway
♦ Quite demanding climb out of Corfe Castle

The route passes through some dramatic scenery and there are some fantastic views, including those of the secluded haven of Encombe House and the Clavel Tower near Kimmeridge.
Nearby attractions include the superb coastal path (strictly for walking), the small village of Kimmeridge and Smedmore House 0929 480717.

[1] Start in one of the lay-bys in Ulwell. Head towards Swanage, take the first road on the right past the entrance to Ulwell Cottage Caravan Park and then right again. At the junction beside the brick works turn right. Shortly after the cemetery turn left. At the next T junction turn right past the school.

[2] Take the rough road on the left near Bonfields Stone that is just before the large road sign. Climb the track until you reach a cattle grid, veer left towards Swanage. After a short distance take the track on the right over a second cattle grid (the bridleway sign is slightly concealed on the left of the gate). Follow the track to the left of South Barn and then behind it, continue along this well worn and well-marked route known as Priests Way to Worth Matravers.

[3] On reaching the road turn left into the village. Exit by the first road on the right past the Square and Compass. At the T junction turn left and follow the road into Kingston. Once in the village turn left and then follow the road to the right of the church towards Encombe House. Continue straight ahead on the metalled road after some distance there are two large pillars on the left pass between these.

[4] Take the bridleway on the right to Swyre Head and then follow the signs to Smedmore Hill and Kimmeridge.* On reaching the road turn left and then right.

[5] At the T junction turn right towards Church Knowle. Take the bridleway on the left to Ridgeway Hill; initially this passes through a field and then onto a small track. Turn left and then sharp right climbing the steep hill. At the top pass through a gate onto a stony track, and turn right towards Cocknowle and Corfe Castle.*

[6] On reaching the road continue straight ahead in order to join the Ridge Path to Corfe Castle, follow the mixture of blue and black arrows until you reach the road near the castle, then turn left.

[7] At the T junction turn right towards Swanage and then take the second road on the left, Sandy Hills Lane, under the railway bridge. Take the bridleway on the left to Ulwell, follow this all the way along the ridge until you reach the road. Turn right returning to the start.

* I have confirmation from Dorset County Council that the track running towards Smedmore Hill and the track running from Ridgeway Hill to Knowle Hill are both unclassified County roads and can therefore be ridden by cyclists.

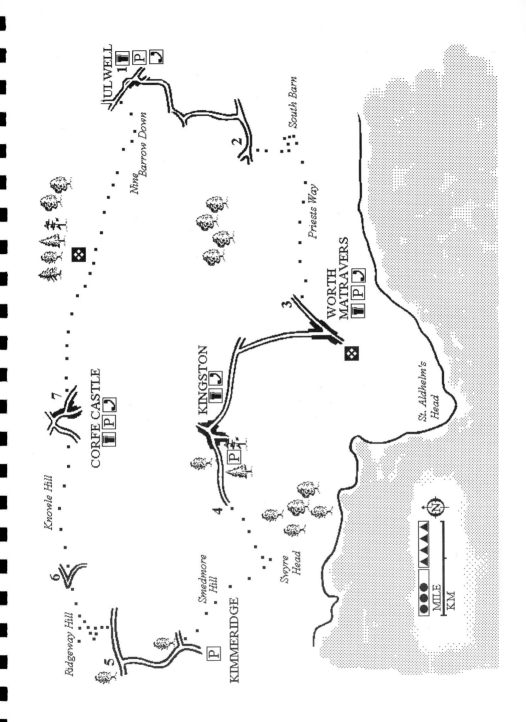

ULWELL

Nine Barrow Down

South Barn

Priests Way

WORTH MATRAVERS

St. Aldhelm's Head

KINGSTON

CORFE CASTLE

Knowle Hill

Smedmore Hill

Swyre Head

Ridgeway Hill

KIMMERIDGE

MILE
KM

15

3. Nine Barrow Down   15/9 miles

START LOCATION AND ACCESS: Corfe Castle is on the A351 between Wareham and Swanage. There are several small car parks, if the village is not very busy leave your vehicle in the large lay-by beneath the castle.
OS MAP REF.: 959825

WARNINGS AND HIGHLIGHTS
♦ Steep and bumpy climb to Nine Barrow Down
♦ Fast descent from the transmission mast into Corfe Castle
♦ Ramblers
♦ Sheep

The route offers some spectacular panoramic views not least from Old Harry across Studland Bay

[1] From the lay-by next to the Castle take the road under the railway bridge to Studland past the water works.

[2] Turn left towards Bushey and the first right through the small village.

[3] At the cross-roads turn left and head in the direction of the forestry plantations, continue along the 'no through road'.

[4] Take the bridleway towards Goathorn, follow the main track ignoring all the side turnings. Continue on the marked bridleway ignoring the track on the left to Goathorn. When the main forestry track ends pass around the metal barrier and continue on the stony track to the road.

[5] Turn right and follow the road into the village of Studland, once there follow the directions to the Bankes Arms. For a shorter alternative take the road straight ahead following the signs towards Swanage, at the foot of the hill before you enter Ulwell take the bridleway on the right to Corfe Castle (instruction 9).

[6] Whiz past the pub down the hill, at the bottom just beyond the public toilets turn left up the slight incline, follow the well-worn track to Old Harry.

[7] The bridleway runs almost parallel to the cliff edge, follow it straight ahead. Ignore the option of veering to the right through the gate, turn right at the end of the meadow on the clearly more popular route up the hill.

[8] Progress past the triangulation pillar to the Obelisk, once there veer right down the steep hill to the road, and turn left.

[9] Shortly after the junction take the bridleway on the right to Corfe Castle. Halfway up the rough and bumpy track take the right fork to Nine Barrow Down. Cycle along the easy to follow trail through the sheep.

[10] Shortly after the transmission mast make the tricky descent to the road, turn right.

[11] Pass under the railway bridge into the village of Corfe Castle.

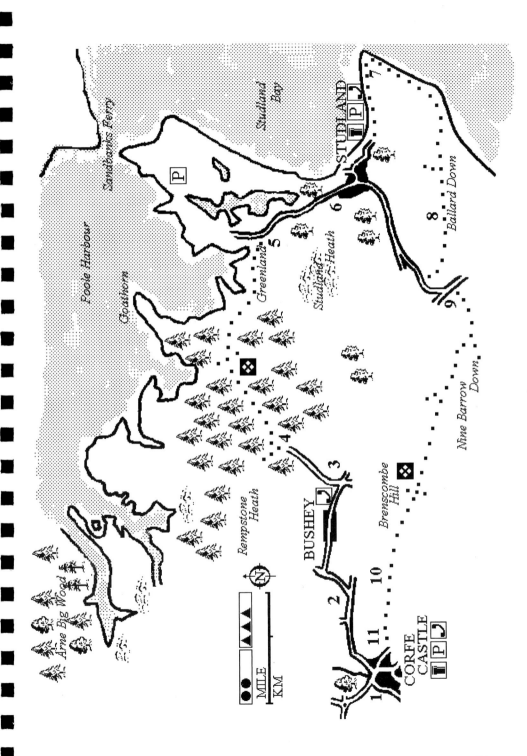

4. Middlebere Heath   11 miles

START LOCATION AND ACCESS: Wareham railway station is on the outskirts of the town and is well sign posted from the A351. There are a number of alternative car parks nearer the town centre.
OS MAP REF.: 919862
NEAREST RAILWAY STATION: Guess!

WARNINGS AND HIGHLIGHTS
- ♦ Blind corners on the road from Arne to Corfe Castle
- ♦ Stiff climb through Cocknowle followed by very fast descent through a tight hairpin bend

[1] From Wareham railway station head through the town centre towards Swanage across the causeway into Stoborough, turn left shortly after the Kings Arms along Nutcrack Lane towards Arne. Cycle straight on through Ridge counting the roads on the right as you go.

Corfe Castle

[2] Take the third road on the right, follow the twisting undulating route to the small roundabout at Norden on the outskirts of Corfe Castle.

[3] Head into Corfe Castle, at the foot of the hill, immediately before the castle, turn right and follow the road to the village of Church Knowle.

[4] Pass through the village and turn right at the cross-roads towards Wareham, climb through the tiny hamlet of Cocknowle.

[5] From the top of the ridge sweep down the hill round the sharp hairpin bend. Continue past Blue Pool to the roundabout at the end of the by pass; take the exit to Wareham through Stoborough.

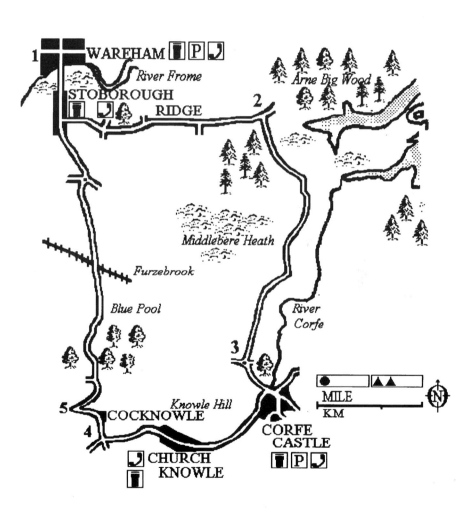

5.   White Horse Hill   20/12 miles

START LOCATION AND ACCESS: Moreton railway station is on the B3390, the road linking the A352 and the A35.
OS MAP REF.: 779891
NEAREST RAILWAY STATION: Moreton

WARNINGS AND HIGHLIGHTS
♦ If the wind blows from the west the very exposed coastal route is gruelling
♦ Narrow access road to NT car park at South Down
♦ Fast bumpy descent towards Broadmayne
♦ Coastal bridleway popular with horse riders and of course ramblers

PUBS
The Frampton Arms	Moreton Station	0305 852253
The Sailors Return	East Chaldon	0305 853847
The Black Dog	Broadmayne	0305 852360

PLACES OF INTEREST
Look out for the strange and intriguing sculptures along the cliff top, the splendid view of Poxwell Manor and of course the White Horse. Nearby attractions include Lulworth Cove and Durdle Door.

[1] Head away from Moreton station towards Crossways, pass the petrol station before taking the next left towards Owermoigne. Turn right immediately before the railway bridge (alternatively if you wish to visit the village of Moreton cross the bridge). At the next junction continue straight ahead passing Tadnoll Mill farm.

[2] At the cross-roads proceed straight ahead to East Chaldon, speed past the Sailors Return before following the road around to the left towards Winfrith Newburgh.

[3] Take the bridleway on the right to Daggers Gate, it is well marked and on the whole easy to follow. A short distance after the large barn complex at the foot of the hill and before reaching the road, turn sharp right along the gravel track.

[4] Continue along the track towards Ringstead and White Nothe; look out for the interesting stone sculptures. Cycle straight ahead towards Falcon Barn and then on through the National Trust car park for South Down to the narrow metalled access road, follow this through Upton to the junction with the main road.

[5] Turn right and cycle along the busy road for approximately 200 metres. Just before the road bends sharply to the left take the bridleway on the left through the small gate (prepare in advance for a stiff climb by dropping into the granny ring).

[6] At the brow of the hill the bridleway is not well defined so head towards the small bush slightly to the right. Pass through the gap and continue straight across the field, through the gates and then follow the well-marked bridleway past the barn.

[7] When the bridleway meets a stony chalk track turn right towards Broadmayne. After approximately 1 mile pass through the small gate on the left and proceed across the field, pass through the gate onto the track and follow this to the road running through Broadmayne.

[8] At the road turn left and then right towards West Knighton. Turn right along Watergates Lane. Continue along the track past the small trout farm and then across the small stream.

[9] At the bridleway T junction turn right, cross the metalled road and continue on into the woods. On reaching the road turn left and return to Moreton station via Crossways.

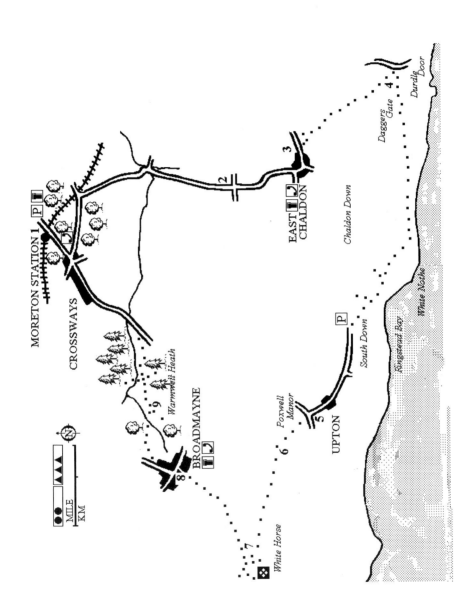

6. Puddletown Forest 18/8 miles

START LOCATION AND ACCESS: Moreton Station is on the B3390, that is the road that links the A352 and the A35.
OS MAP REF.: 779891
NEAREST RAILWAY STATION: Moreton

WARNINGS AND HIGHLIGHTS
♦ River crossing after Lewell Mill
♦ Fast bumpy track through Puddletown Forest is popular with ramblers and people walking dogs
♦ Extremely steep descent from the Briantspuddle road into the forest

PUBS
The Frampton Arms	Moreton Station	0305 852253
The Prince of Wales	Puddletown	0305 848222
The Blue Vinny	Puddletown	0305 848228

PLACES OF INTEREST
Woodsford Castle: 14th century fortified manor house
Thomas Hardy's Cottage: Picturesque birthplace of the famous Dorset writer now owned by the National Trust
Athelhampton House: Tudor manor house. Delightful gardens 0305 848363

It is worth spending some time in the village of Puddletown which has some delightful old cottages off the main road as well as the rather grander large buildings in the centre. Look out for Islington House which is now open to the public.

LINK INFORMATION
The route can easily be combined with the Devil's Brook circuit (23) as they both pass through Puddletown or the White Horse ride (5) as they both commence at Moreton Station.

[1] From Moreton station follow the road past the Frampton Arms. At the next cross-roads turn left towards Dorchester, continue along the road past Woodford Castle.

[2] At the T junction turn right towards West Stafford and then turn right along the no through road to Lewell Mill. At the end of the road pass through the gate and follow the marked bridleway. You will pass over a couple of small bridges and through a small stream before the track runs around the edge of a field.

[3] At the road turn left and then right at the cross-roads towards Higher Bockhampton. Take the next right to Hardy's Cottage. Shortly after passing the cottage take the bridleway to Puddletown - keep straight ahead.

[4] At the end of the track turn left along the metalled bridleway. At the end of the road follow the bridleway directions under the flyover and then along the old road to the right. Take the bridleway on the left up the hill.

[5] At the bridleway T junction turn right and follow the grassy lane until you reach the road, continue into Puddletown and then turn left at the traffic lights towards Milborne St. Andrew. Follow the road past the Blue Vinny Inn and up the hill.

[6] Approximately 1 km after the Inn take the marked bridleway on the right beside the bus stop. Follow the farm access track until you reach a bridleway T junction in the midst of a collection of farm buildings, turn right up the slight incline and follow the track to the road. Turn left and proceed for a few hundred metres, just beyond the entrance to Athelhampton House take the marked bridleway on the right that runs behind the church; the route is well marked with blue arrows. At the road turn left and then right to the village of Affpuddle.

[7] Once in the centre of the village take the marked bridleway on the right, it is opposite the church and beside the telephone box. Continue along the track past a small farm complex before entering the woods through a metal gate. Just before the track begins to climb steeply take the more obscure track on the left up the steeper incline (if you miss the track and reach the forestry access route turn left and follow this to the road). At the top of the climb turn left at the vague bridleway cross-roads on the more clearly defined track and then follow the blue arrows through the forest. Once you are out of the woods take the next track on the right and then at the gravel track turn left. At the road head towards Briantspuddle.

[8] Keep a look out for the marked bridleway on the right (if you reach Culpeppers Dish picnic place turn back) descend the very steep hill with caution. Follow the marked bridleway across the forest track. At the next forest track turn right, from here the bridleway is well marked, follow it to the road and then turn right. At the cross-roads turn left and follow the road back to Moreton station.

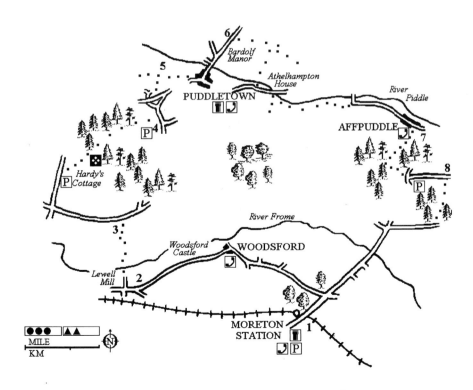

7. Maiden Castle   16/7 miles

START LOCATION AND ACCESS: Maiden Castle is well sign posted on the road out of Dorchester towards Weymouth.
OS MAP REF.: 668889
NEAREST RAILWAY STATION: Dorchester

WARNINGS AND HIGHLIGHTS
♦ Very steep and long climb out of Abbotsbury
♦ Extremely fast descent into Martinstown
♦ The Dorset Coastal Path is very popular with hikers and ramblers - please be considerate and courteous

PUBS

The Kings Arms	Portesham	0305 871342
The Swan Inn	Abbotsbury	0305 871249
Ilchester Arms	Abbotsbury	0305 871243
The Brewers Arms	Martinstown	0305 889361

PLACES OF INTEREST
Maiden Castle: hugely impressive hillfort
The Hardy Monument: architectural carbuncle commemorating the deeds of local hero Admiral Sir Thomas Hardy
Abbotsbury: beautiful village with many attractions including St. Catherines Chapel, the Abbey Barn, the Swannery and the Sub Tropical Gardens

Look out for the many signs of prehistoric life including the proliferation of tumuli between Maiden Castle and the Hardy Monument.

[1] From Maiden Castle car park follow the track that runs beside the outer ramparts. Pass through a gate and continue around the edge of the castle passing through another gate into a more open field. Continue across and pass through a gate onto the road. Go straight ahead and then left at the junction, passing the farm buildings on the right and then up the hill.

[2] At the brow of the hill take the bridleway on the right along the Dorset coastal path to the Hardy Monument

[3] From the monument car park take the bridleway through the wood to West Bexington. Once beyond the trees follow the sign posted bridleway to Portesham. At the road turn right.

[4] At the 'T' junction turn left towards Abbotsbury. At the next 'T' junction, shortly after the King's Arms, turn right onto the busy road towards Bridport. After approximately $\frac{1}{4}$ mile the road turns sharply to the left, do not follow this route, but take the track on the right. Follow the concrete track to the left and then pass through two black metal gates to the right of the farm yard. The bridleway follows the disused railway line and is indicated by a blue arrow. On reaching the road turn left into the village of Abbotsbury.

[5] Leave Abbotsbury on the road to Martinstown past the small chapel and the public toilets. Climb the steep hill passing the Lime Kiln picnic site. Continue straight ahead at the cross-roads and descend the hill past the Hardy Monument. (As an alternative you may wish to retrace your route along the bridleway on the right).

[6] At the 'T' junction turn right into Martinstown. Once through the village turn left. When the road forks take the bridleway on the right and continue along this through a farmyard and eventually back past Maiden Castle to the car park.

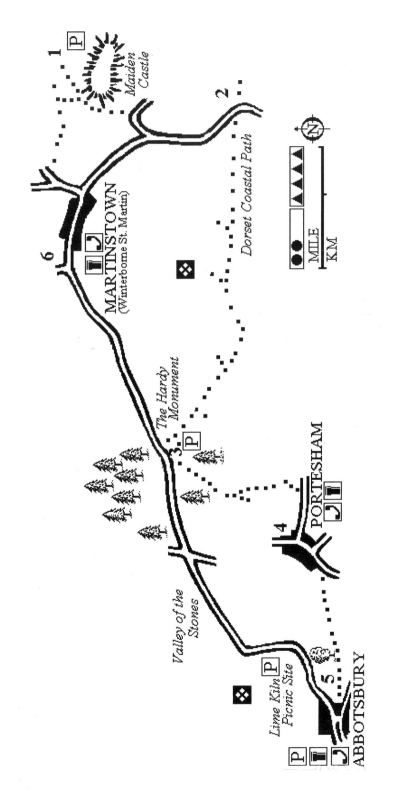

25

Six of the best . . .
viewpoints

There are many fantastic views in Dorset the following are six of my personal favourites.

The Hardy Monument (7 & 8)
Brilliant views towards Abbotsbury, Portland and the coast in the south

Swyre Head (2)
Breathtaking views along the rugged coast

Bulbarrow (21)
The stone near the car park indicates how far it is possible to see when looking out over the pastoral Blackmore Vale.

Pilsdon Pen (11)
The highest point in Dorset offers views over the rural Marshwood Vale towards the coast

Shaftesbury (16)
There are some fantastic views from this historic town especially across the Blackmore Vale

Kingston (2)
Probably the best view of Corfe Castle and the village

Six of the best . . .
road descents

All the following hills present ideal opportunities to go very fast but of course this must be tempered by the paramount need of safety both to you and other road users.

Okeford Hill towards Okeford Fitzpaine (20)
Very fast hill with T junction at the foot of it. Allow plenty of time to stop safely.

Eggardon Hill to Powerstock (9)
Very narrow and rough road that is infrequently used but be prepared to meet oncoming vehicles.

The Hardy Monument to Martinstown (7)
Long gentle slope with plenty of time to slow before the T junction at the bottom.

Descent into Beaminster (11)
Very long and steep hill that gets steeper nearer the town.

Descent towards Ibberton (21)
Very steep and twisty road with several blind corners. Care needs to be exercised.

Ashmore to Washers Pit (19)
Very fast descent, do not whiz past the entrance to the forest.

8. The Hardy Monument   12/5 miles

START LOCATION AND ACCESS: The Hardy Monument can be seen for miles around and is well sign posted from Martinstown which is easily accessed from the A35.
OS MAP REF.: 613877
NEAREST RAILWAY STATION: Dorchester

WARNINGS AND HIGHLIGHTS
♦ Very fast and very bumpy rutted track into Winterborne Abbas
♦ Stiff climb back to the Hardy Monument

PUBS
The Coach and Horses Winterborne Abbas   0305 889340

PLACES OF INTEREST
The Hardy Monument: Erected in memory of local hero, Admiral Sir Thomas Masterman Hardy
Littlebredy: very peaceful and undoubtedly one of the county's most picturesque villages
The Nine Stones, Winterborne Abbas: approximately $\frac{1}{2}$ mile to the west of the village is the mysterious Bronze Age circle of stones. Although it is not exactly Stone Henge there is an eerie atmosphere in spite of the close proximity of the main road.

LINK INFORMATION
As both this route and the Maiden Castle route pass the Hardy Monument it is very simple to combine the two.

[1] Turn right from the Hardy Monument car park down the hill. Take the sign posted bridleway on the left of the gate. Follow the well-worn route through the wood, once you are beyond the trees follow the bumpy track, beside the plantation to the road.

[2] Cross the road and trace the bridleway around the edge of the small copse. At the road turn right and then take the first left. The road passes the picturesque cricket ground before entering the village of Littlebredy. At the junction near the telephone box turn left.

[3] Approximately one mile after the village, and just before the road bends sharply to the left, take the sign posted bridleway on the right. Climb the rough chalky track to the top of the hill.

[4] At the summit pass through the gate into the small enclosed area and then take the bridleway on the left that runs along the edge of the field towards Longbredy Hut and Kingston Russell. At the farm access road turn right.

[5] Cross the busy road with care and then take the right fork, continue past the farm buildings.

[6] At the junction turn right and proceed along the road to Dorchester for approximately $1\frac{1}{2}$ miles before taking the marked bridleway on the right. Head across the field diagonally to the left towards a large barn where the bridleway joins a stony track, follow this carefully down the hill to the main road running through Winterborne Abbas.

[7] Turn left and then right to Winterborne Steepleton, proceed through the village towards Martinstown.

[8] Take the bridleway on the right near the slightly concealed signs for Lower Rew and Sunnydale Farm. Climb the bumpy track until it reaches the road and then turn right to complete the ascent to the Hardy Monument.

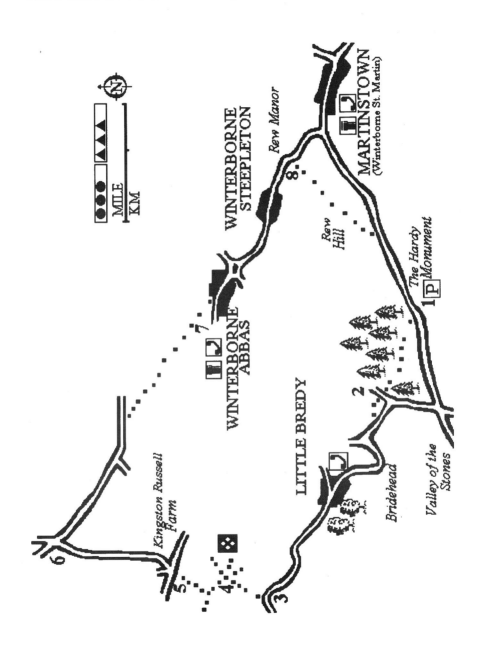

9.   Eggardon Hill

19/2 miles

START LOCATION AND ACCESS: Shatcombe Lane runs from Wynford Eagle to Eggardon Hill, the picnic site is very near the hill fort which is well sign posted and easily reached from the A35(T) or the A356.

OS MAP REF.: 548948

NEAREST RAILWAY STATION: Maiden Newton

WARNINGS AND HIGHLIGHTS

♦ Several arduous climbs, especially out of Hooke
♦ Several very fast descents including into Powerstock and the return towards Hooke
♦ Narrow roads with several blind corners
♦ Poor road surfaces
♦ Sunday drivers wearing hats

PUBS

The Three Horseshoes	Powerstock	030 885 328
The Old Swan	Toller Porcorum	0300 20391

PLACES OF INTEREST

Eggardon Hill: spectacular windswept Iron Age hill fort that has an eerie atmosphere
Mapperton Manor: good looking manor house whose charming formal gardens are open to the public. 0308 862645
Hooke Park: beautiful woodlands that are part of the Parnham Trust enterprize. 0308 863130
Kingcombe Meadows: a pleasant area that is of special scientific interest.

LINK INFORMATION

To join the Batcombe Hill route take the road from Rampisham to Evershot.

[1] Start with the Shatcombe Lane picnic site behind you, head off to the right and then left towards Askerswell. Turn right to Powerstock past Eggardon Hill down the very steep hill, but be cautious of any on coming traffic on this narrow road.

[2] Cycle past the Three Horseshoes and then straight ahead at the junction along the road that is not sign posted past a house with lions on its gateposts. At the fork proceed to the right, turn left at the T junction and then take the next left.

[3] Take the next right to Loscombe, pass through the tiny village and then climb the hill that is overhung by trees.

[4] Turn right at the T junction.

[5] Shortly after passing Mapperton Manor take the right fork to Coltleigh Farm.

[6] Pass through the farm buildings and continue along the marked bridleway passing through 3 gates before reaching the road; turn right.

[7] Just after the entrance to Hooke Park turn left and descend into the village of Hooke itself.

[8] Turn left immediately after the church to the main road A356. You will shortly appreciate why your bike has so many gears as you climb the awesome hill.

[9] At the junction cross the busy road with care and join the marked bridleway directly opposite, follow this across the large fields to a gate in the distant hedge, turn right.

[10] At the next T junction turn right towards Wraxall. Once in the village of Rampisham turn right and climb past the church.

[11] Head straight on at the cross-roads towards Kingcombe and then at the foot of the fast descent turn left towards Toller and Lower Kingcombe.

[12] Pass through the village of Toller Pocorum turning right at the junction beside the Old Swan towards Askerswell.

[13] At Barrowland Lane junction turn left and continue towards Askerswell, take the next left returning to the picnic site.

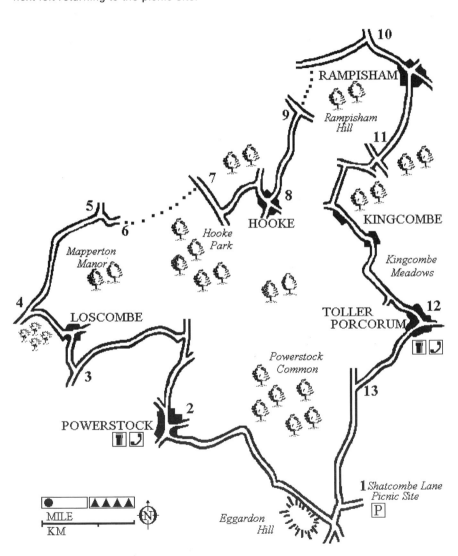

10. Lambert's Castle   13/5 miles

START LOCATION AND ACCESS: The National Trust car park at Langdon Hill is easily reached from the A35(T) between Morcombelake and Chideock.
OS MAP REF.: 413932
NEAREST RAILWAY STATION: Axminster

WARNINGS AND HIGHLIGHTS
♦ Very hilly route
♦ Narrow roads with blind corners
♦ Very fast and potentially dangerous bumpy track between (8) and (9)

PUBS
The Five Bells   Whitchurch Canonicorum   0297 89262

PLACES OF INTEREST
Golden Cap estate: an extremely beautiful stretch of coastland owned by the National Trust popular with walkers. Golden Cap is the highest sea cliff on the south coast. Lambert's Castle and Coney's Castle: two hill forts in close proximity to each other on the edge of the Marshwood Vale, both are owned by the National Trust and were previously owned by several iron maiden fans.

Look out for St. Wite's Well, the mock tudor manor house in Catheston Leweston and the fantastic views over the beautiful pastoral scenery of the Marshwood Vale. Nearby attractions include the traditional seaside resort of Charmouth and the very tempting Old Moores Biscuit factory.

[1] Start in the National Trust car park at Langdon Hill. Follow the access road back to the entrance and turn left towards Filcombe, Norchard and Upcot Farms.

[2] At Pickaxe Cross turn right. Follow the track past St Wites' Well until you meet a small road; turn left. After a while the road becomes a track; follow this until you reach a set of gates. Pass through the metal gate to the left of the yellow post. Climb the hill on the gravel track.

[3] At the top follow the stony access road sign posted to Charmouth; continue in the same direction down the steep and narrow metalled road.

[4] At the foot of the hill turn left on the main road towards Charmouth. Take the next turning on the right to Catherston Leweston; continue through the village to Wootton Fitzpaine.

[5] At the T junction near Knapp Farm turn left towards Monkton Wyld and continue straight ahead at the next junction towards Lambert's Castle. Follow the road around to the left towards Fishponds.

[6] Take the marked bridleway on the left. Follow the bumpy track past Marsh Farm. Approximately $\frac{1}{4}$ mile past the farm buildings follow the track sharply to the right into the forest. On reaching the forestry track turn left and then left again at the road.

[7] At the next junction continue straight ahead along the stony track beside the whitewashed cottage. At the top of the hill turn right.

[8] At Peters Gore junction take the marked bridleway past Gypsies End. Take care it is a particularly bumpy descent until the farmyard is reached. At the road turn right.

[9] At Wootton Cross junction turn left towards Whitchurch. On reaching the cross-roads in Whitchurch Canonicorum turn left towards Shave Cross; continue past the phone box and the church. Follow the signs to Ryall past The Five Bells.

[10] Once in Ryall follow the road towards Bridport. At the junction with the main road turn left. At the top of the hill turn right immediately before the 'try your brakes' sign. Follow the access road back to the car park.

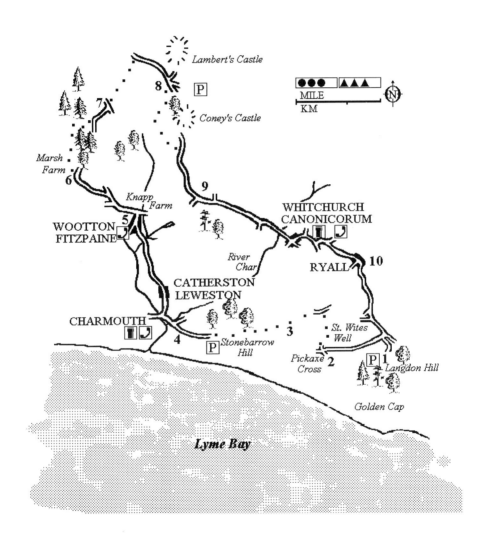

11. Pilsdon Pen   22 miles

START LOCATION AND ACCESS: Beaminster is easily reached from Bridport on the A3066 or from Dorchester on the A356. There is a large car park that is very easy to find.
OS MAP REF.: 482013
NEAREST RAILWAY STATION: Crewkerne

WARNINGS AND HIGHLIGHTS
♦ Very hilly stamina saping route
♦ There are some very uneven road surfaces including a particularly rough stretch across Knowle Hill
♦ Lots of blind corners on the narrow little used roads, many of which have high hedges
♦ Extremely fast descent into Beaminster

PUBS
The New Inn	Stoke Abbot	0308 68333
The White Lion	Broadwindsor	0308 68855
The Cross Keys	Broadwindsor	0308 68434
The Winyards Gap Inn	Cheddington	0935 891244
The Fox	Corscombe	0935 891330

PLACES OF INTEREST
Beaminster: small bustling town with many interesting buildings and it's fair share of interesting pubs, cafes and restaurants. A popular nearby attraction is Parnham House just outside of the town 0308 862204.
Pilsdon Pen: another des. res. of those hairy individuals of the Iron Age with superb views - this is not surprizing as it is the highest point in Dorset. Owned by the NT.
The route passes through some of the county's most beautiful scenery and tranquil peaceful villages. There is much to admire however, many of the roads are very narrow and it is essential that your concentration is not too distracted from the road.

[1] From the centre of Beaminster take the road towards Broadwindsor. Turn left to Stoke Abbott and then continue through the village towards Bridport.

[2] At the cross-roads proceed straight ahead towards Shave Cross and Whitchurch down the narrow and potentially very fast hill. Turn right towards Pilsdon. At the next junction head towards Broadwindsor and Beaminster.

[3] At the T junction, in the shadow of Pilsdon Pen, turn right to Broadwindsor.

[4] In Broadwindsor follow the one-way road beside the White Lion to Beaminster and Mosterton. Turn left towards Mosterton and then take the next left to Little Windsor.

[5] At the T junction in Littlewindsor turn left towards Drimpton and then the next left to Seaborough. Continue straight ahead at the next junction towards Misterton. Once you have reached the village of Seaborough turn right past the small post box towards Misterton. Proceed along this road until you reach a junction with a small triangle of grass upon which there is Somerset County Council sign, turn right. Follow this very bumpy road until you reach the main road running through the village of Mosterton.

[6] Turn right and then left to Cheddington and Halstock. Continue along this road until you see the access road to Broadleaze Farm on your right, take the narrow road on the left down the steep gorge opposite. Pass through the village of Cheddington to the junction at Winyards Gap.

[7] Cross the busy road with care and head towards Halstock, take the next right to Corscombe. Turn right at the T junction and then right again at the junction beside the stables to leave the village.

[8] At the cross-roads go straight ahead to Beaminster.

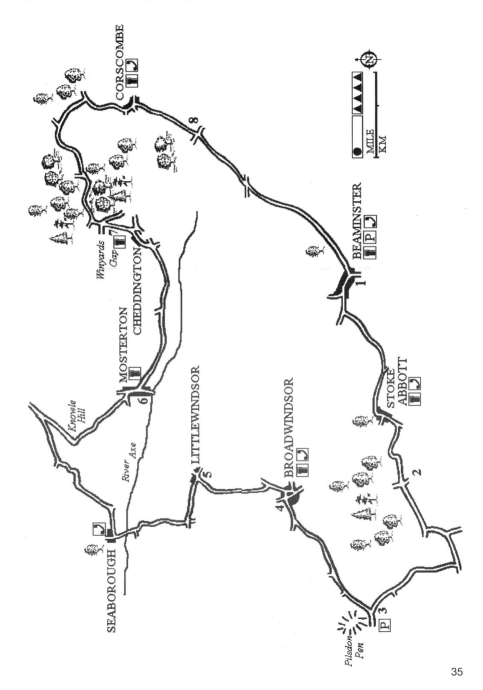

12.   Sydling Water   13/8 miles

START LOCATION AND ACCESS: Batcombe Hill picnic site is on the road between Evershot and Minterne Magna i.e. the road between the A37 and the A352.
OS MAP REF.: 637039
NEAREST RAILWAY STATION: Maiden Newton

WARNINGS AND HIGHLIGHTS
♦ Long fast bumpy descent towards Higher City Farm
♦ Stiff climb from Upper Sydling

PUBS
The Smith's Arms   Godmanstone   0300 341236
The Greyhound Inn   Sydling St. Nicholas   0300 341303

PLACES OF INTEREST
The Smith's Arms is one of the smallest pubs in the country and dates from the 17th century.
Sydling St. Nicholas is a very pretty village well worth looking around.
The Cross and Hand: small stone pillar on the edge of the road may have been a Saxon boundary marker.

LINK INFORMATION
To connect with Piddle Valley route turn right on the road just before Higher City Farm (3) and follow the road into Cerne Abbas.

[1] Leave Batcombe Hill picnic site by turning right onto the road. Take the bridleway on the left directly opposite the turning to the Friary. On reaching the stony track continue to the left.

[2] Follow the track around to the right alongside the wire fence. Ignore the turning to the right and proceed straight ahead along the more bumpy track that will eventually take you past a transmission mast on the left.

[3] Cross the road and follow the marked bridleway past Higher City Farm. The bridleway is well marked and after passing through several gates you will pass a small wood that it is possible to enter by a stile. This is a tranquil area littered with rocks where daffodils grow in the spring, there are also some curious sculptures. If you wish to visit Godmanstone turn left beyond the wood through the gate and down the hill (to return to the main route turn right onto the road and continue for a short distance before turning left along the bridleway to Sydling), otherwise continue straight on.

[4] After passing through a gate and observing the polite instructions you will reach a fork, take the right prong down the hill on the stony track. At the sharp hairpin leave the track and follow the grassy bridleway to the small gate beside some trees.

[5] Follow the marked bridleway diagonally to the right across the field. Pass through the small wooden gate and then descend the short steep hill past a small tree plantation. At the base of the hill continue to the left along the valley bottom heading for a cottage and some farm buildings. Pass through the gate and past the buildings to the road.

[6] Turn right and follow the road through Sydling St. Nicholas at the cross-roads beyond the village go straight on to Up Sydling. Immediately after crossing the cobbles turn left alongside the stream.

[7] Turn left across the stream beside the entrance to Upper Sydling House. Proceed along the chalky track past the barns at the next junction turn right remaining on the chalky track as it curves to the left and then gradually climbs the hill. Near to the brow of the hill keep to the right of the brick barn and then follow the track past a disused observation tower on the left before reaching the road.

[8] Turn right and then right again at the T junction towards the Friary, follow the road back to the picnic site.

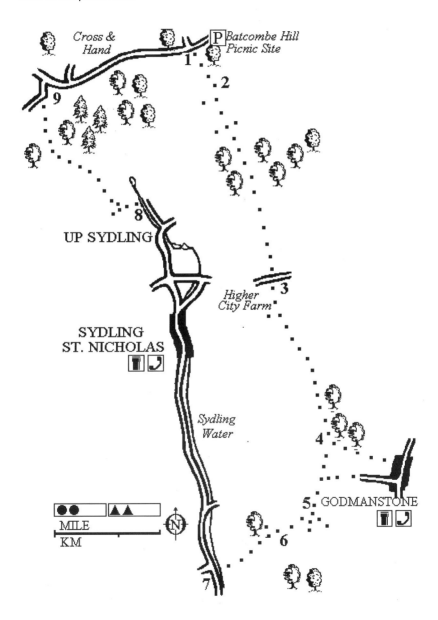

13. Batcombe Hill   20/1 miles

START LOCATION AND ACCESS: Batcombe Hill is on the road between Evershot and Minterne Magna i.e. the road between the A37 and the A352.
OS MAP REF.: 637039
NEAREST RAILWAY STATION: Maiden Newton or Chetnole

WARNINGS AND HIGHLIGHTS
♦ Hilly route, especially demanding climb past The Friary to Batcome Hill picnic site.
♦ Narrow uneven roads with several blind corners

PUBS
The Acorn Hotel	Evershot	0935 83228
The Chetnole Inn	Chetnole	0935 872337
The Carpenters Arms	Leigh	0935 872438

PLACES OF INTEREST
The Cross and Hand: weather beaten stone pillar that may be a Saxon boundary marker.
Evershot: very pleasant stone village.
Look out for the many attractive buildings on this route and the small ancient earthwork slightly off the route in Leigh known as the Miz Maze.

LINK INFORMATION
This route and the Sydling Water route link naturally as they both have the same start location however, it is also very easy to join the Eggardon Hill ride. At the Sandhills junction take the left fork and follow the road through the village of Wraxall to Rampisham turn right past the church and follow the route instructions.

[1] Leave Batcombe Hill picnic site by turning right. Take the first road on the left, but only to gain immediate access to the track on the right, follow this bridleway to the busy A37. Turn right and then after a short distance take the marked bridleway on the left along the gravel track.

[2] On reaching the road turn left, proceed to follow the road through the village of Frome St. Quintin.

[3] At the junction beyond the orchard on the left, turn right towards Maiden Newton. At the next T junction turn right, cross the railway bridge and then take the road to Evershot. Continue straight ahead until you reach a T junction, turn right and follow the road through the village of Evershot to the junction with the A37 upon which there is a considerable amount of construction work taking place and you may therefore experience some problems and extra care should be exercised.

[4] Turn right and then left towards Batcombe and Minterne Magna and then left again to Chetnole (A shorter alternative is to continue straight on following the road directly to Batcombe Hill). Pass through the tunnel and then turn left at the next T junction into the village of Chetnole.

[5] At the junction near the church turn right past The Chetnole Inn to Leigh, continue past the Carpenters Arms before turning right at the T junction towards Sherborne and Cerne Abbas and then follow the road towards Hermitage and Hillfield.

[6] Turn right and then next left to the Friary. At the next T junction turn left towards Evershot, at the top of the very steep hill turn left and return to the picnic site.

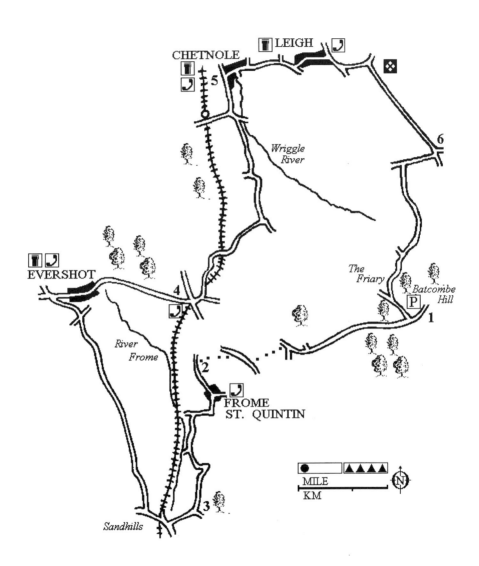

CHETNOLE

LEIGH

EVERSHOT

FROME
ST. QUINTIN

The
Friary

Batcombe
Hill

Wriggle
River

River
Frome

Sandhills

MILE

KM

39

Six of the best . . .
Pubs

Although I'm sure it would be a worthwhile challenge I have not visited all the pubs on the routes in this guide however, I have visited quite a number and the following six are personal favourites.

The Acorn Inn Evershot (6)
A charming pub that has a good range of beer and quite excellent food. It may be best to visit after a ride.

The Drovers Inn Gussage All Saints (18)
The beer garden provides an ideal location to eat and drink on a hot summers day.

The Three Horseshoes Powerstock (9)
A splendid pub in a splendid setting that offers splendid food and ale.

The Scott Arms Kingston (2)
There can be few pubs that offer such a beautiful view.

The Rose and Crown Trent (14)
Another pub offering good food and good beer as well as a beer garden.

The Brace of Pheasants Plush (22)
Good food and beer in a delightful setting.

The Brace of Pheasants, Plush

The Scott Arms, Kingston

14. Sherborne   15/1 miles

START LOCATION AND ACCESS: Sherborne lies between Yeovil and Shaftesbury on the A30. The railway station is well sign posted within the town.
OS MAP REF.: 641162
NEAREST RAILWAY STATION: Sherborne

WARNINGS AND HIGHLIGHTS
♦ Narrow roads and blind corners
♦ Very speedy twisty descent into Sandford Orcas on a very loose slippery surface

PUBS
The Mitre Inn	Sandford Orcas	0963 22271
The Rose and Crown	Trent	0935 850776

PLACES OF INTEREST
Sherborne is one of the county's most charming towns and it is well worth taking time to explore. There are many very fine buildings including both castles and arguably Dorset's finest church. There are several pubs and restaurants.
Sandford Orcas Manor House: 16th century manor house. 0963 22206
Worldwide Butterflies and Lullingstone Silk Farm: 0935 74608

The villages on this route are all very appealing in particular look out for the attractive stone buildings in the village of Trent.

[1] From the railway station cycle across the level crossing, at the T junction turn left towards the Shaftesbury road. Proceed past the entrance to the castle, over the railway bridge and then right at the cross-roads.

[2] At the next T junction turn right onto the A30 and then take the next left to Poyntington.

[3] From Poyntington follow the signs to Sandford Orcas, after the fast and tricky descent into the village turn right at the T junction and then left to Trent.

[4] Take the next left past the nursery greenhouses.

[5] Cycle through the village of Trent, past the church to Over Compton.

[6] At the cross-roads turn left to Never Compton.

[7] At the T junction turn right towards Stallen.

[8] At the cross-roads next to the small barn and Court Ash Cottage turn left along the no through road. Climb the steep hill between the narrow cutting and continue straight ahead along the bridleway. When the metalled surface ends, shortly after a track joins the lane from the left, take the bridleway on the right down the hill between the hedges.

[9] At the bottom of the hill cross the dual carriage way carefully and cycle to the right for approximately 200 metres and then turn left down the minor road. At the T junction turn left, continue straight on at the cross-roads into the town and then follow the signs back to the station.

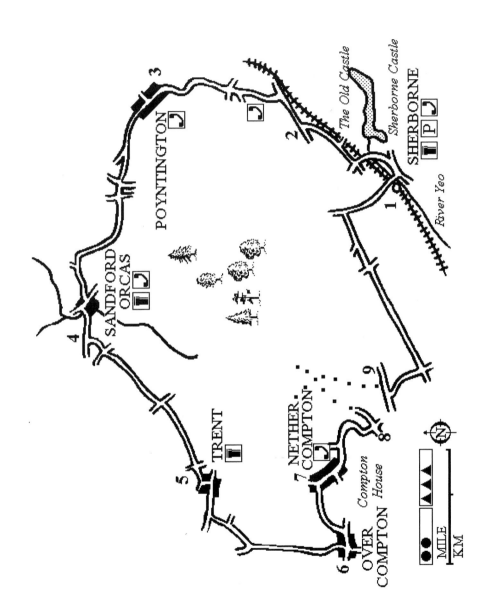

15. Northern Stour Valley   15 miles

START LOCATION AND ACCESS: Gillingham is well sign posted in the north of the county and easily reached from Shaftesbury and Mere. The railway station is well sign posted in the town.
OS MAP REF.: 810261
NEAREST RAILWAY STATION: Gillingham

WARNINGS AND HIGHLIGHTS
♦ Quiet roads

PUBS
The Stapleton Arms	Buckhorn Weston	0963 70396
The Kings Arms Inn	East Stour	0747 838325

PLACES OF INTEREST
Look out for the Woodlands Trust wood and the ancient Trill Bridge as you meander through the pretty villages that nestle within this tranquil valley.

[1] After exiting the car park at the railway station turn left towards Wincanton.

[2] At the traffic lights turn left again towards Wincanton and then left to Buckhorn Weston; on the way pass through Quarr Cross before reaching the village. Continue past the Stapleton Arms and on under the railway bridge.

[3] Turn left towards Gillingham and follow the road into the tiny village of Kington Magna. Wriggle through the small community and climb past the church, at the next cross-roads turn right towards Marnhull.

[4] At the cross-roads continue straight ahead to Fifehead Magdelen passing the Woodlands Trust wood. Turn left at the T junction to Stour Provost, and left again shortly after crossing Trill Bridge.

[5] Take the next right to Woodville, continue past the school and turn left, then right and then left again. At the junction next to Newgate Farm turn left.

[6] At the Kings Arms turn left and then right along Browns Lane to the Crown Inn, turn right.

[7] At Madjeston turn left towards Kington Magna and then right under the railway arch; follow the road around to the right through the attractive new housing estate. At the T junction turn right and then follow the signs back to the railway station.

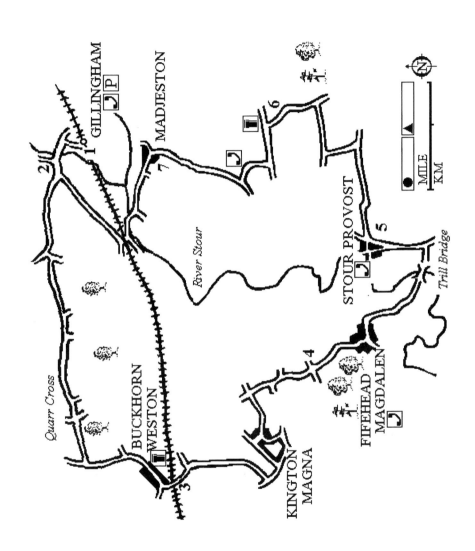

GILLINGHAM

MADJESTON

BUCKHORN
WESTON

Quarr Cross

River Stour

STOUR PROVOST

KINGTON
MAGNA

FIFEHEAD
MAGDALEN

Trill Bridge

MILE
KM

16.   Shaftesbury   16 miles

START LOCATION AND ACCESS: There is a good network of A roads in north Dorset and Shaftesbury is well sign posted and easily located. The information centre is very easy to find in the town centre near a large car park which is clearly signed.
OS MAP REF.: 865230
NEAREST RAILWAY STATION: Gillingham

WARNINGS AND HIGHLIGHTS
♦ Although entirely on tarmac the route is very testing with several fast descents and gruelling climbs, especially the return into Shafesbury

PUBS
The Crown Inn   Fontmell Magna   0747 811441

PLACES OF INTEREST
Shaftesbury is an historic hill fort town that appears to be an ideal venue for a pub crawl. An interesting town with several tourist attractions not least of course Gold Hill, it's easy to see why the lad in the Hovis advert is pushing his bike up the hill.
Melbury Abbas Mill. 0747 2163
Fontmell Down: spectacular scenery maintained by the National Trust.

A very hilly route through some beautiful countryside with many fine views.

[1] From the information centre in the centre of Shaftesbury take the road to the hospital, continue down St. John's Hill and then on past the church.

[2] After approximately 1 mile the road forks, take the left prong and follow the twisting road into the tiny village of Twyford.

[3] Turn left at the junction next to the village sign. On reaching the junction with the busy main road (with the bus stop on your right) turn left down the quiet road; at Corahill cross-roads turn right.

[4] At West Melbury junction continue straight across, follow the road past the telephone box down the hill into the village of Melbury Abbas.

[5] At the T junction turn left along the road towards Blandford up the 1:6 hill, continue past the National Trust car park for Fontmell Down.

[6] Turn right and plummet down the hill through Spinghead to Fontmell Magna.

[7] At the cross-roads continue straight ahead past the Crown Inn and then on past St. Andrew's First School. At the next cross-roads continue straight ahead and ignore all turnings.

[8] When you reach a slightly peculiar offset cross-roads turn right towards Shaftesbury past the Kingdom Hall. Take the next left towards Margaret Marsh and proceed straight ahead until you reach the T junction at Stour Row.

[9] Turn right to Shaftesbury. At the next junction turn right and then follow the sign post which fore warns (as if you hadn't realised) of the rigours to come - very steep hill. At the junction next to the church turn left and continue the climb up St. John's Hill. Follow the road back to the car park.

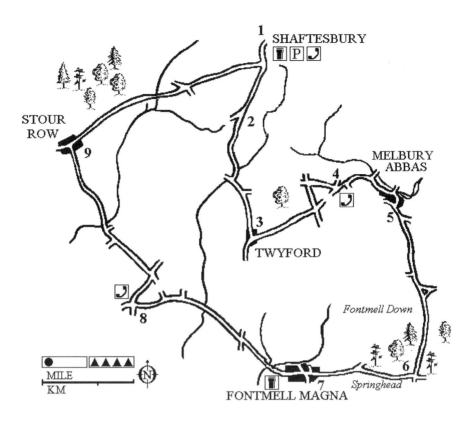

STOUR ROW

SHAFTESBURY

MELBURY ABBAS

TWYFORD

Fontmell Down

FONTMELL MAGNA

Springhead

MILE
KM

Gold Hill, Shaftesbury

17. Cranborne Chase 19/10 miles

START LOCATION AND ACCESS: Cranborne is on the B3078 between Wimborne and Salisbury, the car park is near the school in Water Lane.
OS MAP REF.: 056134

WARNINGS AND HIGHLIGHTS
♦ Very fast bumpy descents towards Pentridge and then into Wimborne St. Giles
♦ Bridleways between Pentridge and Sixpenny Handley tend to be overgrown during the summer months

PUBS
Fleur de Lys Hotel	Cranborne	07254 248
The Sheaf of Arrows	Cranborne	07254 456
The Star Inn	Sixpenny Handley	0725 52272
The Roebuck Inn	Sixpenny Handley	0725 52002
The Bull Inn	Wimborne St. Giles	07254 284

PLACES OF INTEREST
Cranborne Manor: interesting looking manor house not open to the public but whose highly regarded gardens are. 07254 248
Knowleton Church: ghostly church ruins encircled by a neolithic earthwork - one of my favourite haunts
Edmondsham House: constructed in 1589 the house is often open to the public. 07254 207

Look out for the many signs of prehistoric life, ancient settlements and tumuli abound. Don't miss the attractive church and almshouses and quaint stocks in Wimborne St. Giles.

LINK INFORMATION
The route can easily be combined with the Gussage circuit in Wimborne St. Giles.

[1] Exit the car park on the road past the fire station and then take the road to Boveridge. Continue past the Sheath of Arrows and then out of the village.

[2] Take the bridleway on the left to Pentridge along the road not suitable for motor vehicles, at the end of the tarmac pass around the gate onto the well worn track. Follow the undulating track straight ahead.

[3] At the top of the hill pass through the wooden gate and descend the hill alongside the edge of the field. Pass through another gate onto a bumpy track.

[4] At the foot of the hill turn left almost certainly through a large deep puddle. Follow the track around to the right, continue beside the hedge on the right side of the field. At the brow of the hill follow the bridleway towards the service station buildings in the distance, once reached pass through the small gate into the garage forecourt.

[5] Cross the busy road. Pass through the gate into the field and follow the bridleway to the right around the edge of the field. Cross the minor road and pass through the small gate onto the rough, and in places overgrown, bridleway that runs between the two fields. Follow this until you reach the stony track, up to the road and turn left.

[6] At the cross-roads turn right towards Tollard Royal, continue past the Star Inn and then the Roebuck Inn until you reach the junction beside the school. Take the track opposite beside Park Cottage. After approximately $\frac{1}{2}$ mile take the left fork.

[7] Take the next left along the bridleway marked Chapel Down Farm Private Road. Cross the road onto the bridleway directly opposite. Continue straight ahead at the next bridleway cross-roads and on through the small wood onto the gravel track. At the 'T' junction turn right and then almost immediately left. Descend the fast stony track past the farm buildings. At the road continue straight ahead past the Bull Inn.

[8] Follow signs to Gussage All Saints at the 'T' junction. Take the next left turn towards Knowlton Church. At the 'T' junction turn right and then the next left to Woodlands. At the cross-roads continue straight ahead past the farm shop.

[9] At the next 'T' junction turn left towards Edmondsham and right at the next junction. Turn left at the junction near the house gates. Follow the road back to Cranborne.

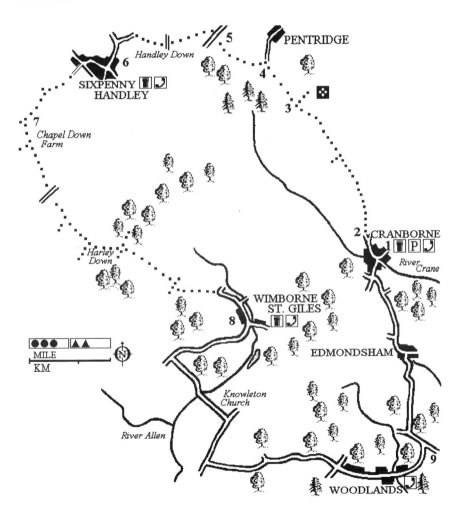

18. Gussage All Saints   7/3 miles

START LOCATION AND ACCESS: Gussage All Saints is easily reached from the A354 (Blandford/Salisbury road) or the B3078 (Wimborne/Salisbury road).
OS MAP REF.: 999108

WARNINGS AND HIGHLIGHTS
♦ Drag to Harley Down
♦ Quite fast descent from Harley Down
♦ Dogs and their owners

PUBS

The Drovers Inn	Gussage All Saints	0258 840084
The Bull Inn	Wimborne St. Giles	07254 284

PLACES OF INTEREST
Both of the villages the route passes through are attractive. In particular look out for the Mill House, stocks, the church and the almshouses in Wimborne St. Giles. The bridleway north through Harley Down passes along the old Roman Road - the Ackling Dyke.

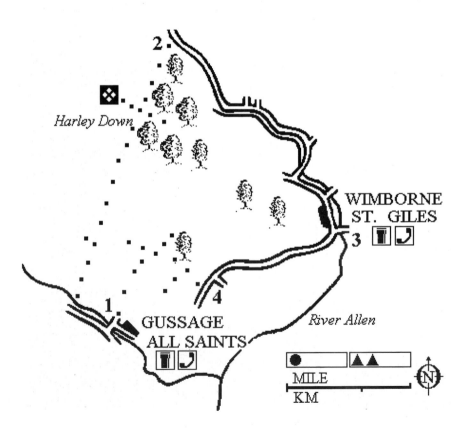

[1] From near the church head out of the village over the small stream and around to the right. Take the bridleway on the right to Harley Down, beside the water pumping station.

[2] On reaching the road turn right and follow the winding road into the village of Wimborne St. Giles.

[3] At the T junction shortly after the Bull Inn turn right towards Gussage All Saints.

[4] Approximately 250 metres after the turning on the left to Knowleton Church take the unmarked bridleway on the right. Continue straight ahead until you reach the bridleway cross-roads at the foot of the hill. Turn left following the track back to the village of Gussage All Saints.

Gussage All Saints Church
(note the old oil lamp)

19. Pimperne   21/8 miles

START LOCATION AND ACCESS: The village of Pimperne is on the A354 between Blandford and Salisbury. St. Peter's church lies on the main road through the village from the A354.
OS MAP REF.: 904094

WARNINGS AND HIGHLIGHTS
♦ The bridleways are infrequently used and therefore tend to be a little overgrown in the summer
♦ Very fast descent out of Ashmore

PUBS

The Anvil Inn	Pimperne	0258 453431
The Farquarson Arms	Pimperne	0258 453115
The Bugle Inn	Tarrant Gunville	025 889 300
The Museum Hotel	Farnham	0725 516261

PLACES OF INTEREST
Chettle House: 18th century house. 0258 89209
Ashmore: picturesque village that is Dorset's highest.
Look out for Eastbury House in Tarrant Gunville.

LINK INFORMATION
This ride can be extended by connecting it to the Tarrant Valley route, full instructions are contained in that route description.

[1] Start with St. Peter's church behind you, head off to your left. Take the first right, Arlecks Lane, continue straight past the tiny industrial estate. When the metalled road surface ends turn left along the stony track.

[2] Continue past the wood, at the bridleway cross-roads turn right and follow the track down the hill past Home Farm.

[3] At the road junction continue straight ahead to Tarrant Gunville. At the T junction turn right toward Tarrant Hinton past the Bugle Inn on the right and then Eastbury House on the left.

[4] At the next junction turn left along the no through road, which after a short distance joins a bridleway. At the bridleway junction follow the track around to the left, pass through a gate and take the right fork.

[5] On reaching a more open area the bridleway heads straight across a meadow to a chalk track near the entrance to a small caravan site. Continue on the track past the entrance to Chettle House and then the church.

[6] At the T junction turn left, pedal past the village store and follow the road to Farnham.

[7] At the T junction beside The Museum Hotel turn left and follow the directions into the village of Ashmore.

[8] Once through Ashmore descend the very steep hill.

[9] At the foot of the hill take the bridleway on the left through Washers Pit towards Stubhampton. Follow the forest track, it forks twice, on each occasion go right. At the edge of the forest proceed along the narrow bridleway through the small copse and then onto a stony track along the steep sided valley bottom.

[10] On reaching the road turn right up the hill. (An easier way is to cycle through Stubhampton and then retrace your route back to Pimperne.) At the brow ignore the bridleway on the left and carry on for approx. 250 metres and then take the marked bridleway on the left next to the metal gate. Follow the twisting route through the trees to an open field, continue on the uneven bridleway along the edge of the field to the road, turn right. At the top of the hill take the second track on the left.

[11] Continue along the track past the stable barn and down the fast bumpy track to the road. Turn right at the next junction and follow the road back into Pimperne.

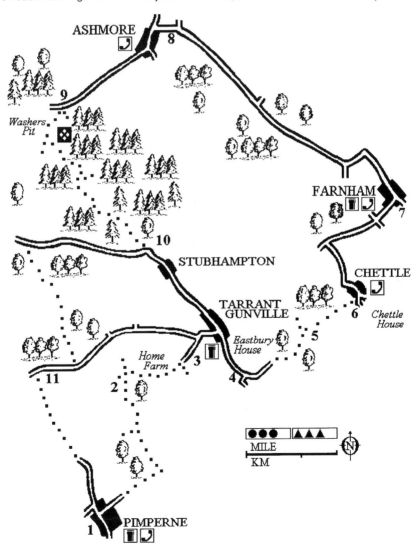

20. Hambledon Hill 17/8 miles

START LOCATION AND ACCESS: Okeford Hill picnic site is on the road between Okeford Fitzpaine (sign posted off the A357) and Winterborne Stickland (easily reached from the A354).
OS MAP REF.: 813093

WARNINGS AND HIGHLIGHTS
♦ Lung bursting climb out of Durweston
♦ Potentially extremely fast descent from Okeford Hill, take care to allow plenty of breaking distance
♦ Some areas prone to glutinous mud, especially near the river

PUBS
The Royal Oak	Okeford Fitzpaine	0258 860308
Saxon Inn	Child Okeford	0258 860310
Bakers Arms	Child Okeford	0258 860260
The White Horse Inn	Stourpaine	0258 453535

PLACES OF INTEREST
Fiddleford Manor: restored 14th century manor house. 0272 734472
Hambledon Hill: superb windswept hill fort with fantastic views.
Hod Hill: another splendid example of the labours of the iron men and maidens with later alterations by the Romans.

[1] Leave the Okeford Hill picnic site car park and turn left down the hill; at the T junction turn right to Okeford Fitzpaine.

[2] At the Royal Oak turn left and then right down Darknoll Lane, ignore the fork to the right and continue along the bumpy and technically testing track.

[3] On reaching the road junction turn left up the hill past the black barn on your left. Near the top of the hill take the marked bridleway on the right into the wood. The bridleway through Piddles Wood is mostly well sign posted however, when you are almost through the wood (you will hear the hum of the traffic on the road) care needs to be exercised. A right angled turn to the left down a slippery slope is concealed and easy to miss, turn back if you reach a wire fence.

[4] At the road turn right with care and then left towards Fiddleford Manor. Turn right at the next T junction and then left along a stony track beside some farm buildings. Turn right along the disused railway track and then take the marked bridleway on the left; follow this over a small wooden bridge across a field and then through a gate onto a track, turn right.

[5] At the road turn left and continue through the small village of Hammoon. At the T junction turn right to Child Okeford. Cycle through the village until you reach the junction near the war memorial, turn sharp left towards Irwerne Minster past the Foxdale Pottery.

[6] After a short distance turn right along the gravel track, this route is very shady and after poor weather has the consistency of partially set blancmange. At the top of the hill pass through the small gate and follow the bridleway straight ahead between the two fields. After approximately 150 metres turn right to the hill fort. Pass through the gate and follow the directions of the Nature Conservancy Council along the well worn, but in places tricky bridleway.

[7] Pass through a small gate and follow the track to the triangulation pillar, turn left down the rough track.

[8] At the foot of the hill turn right and cycle alongside the boundary wall. At the end of the wall turn left and then right beside the trees and past the white sign indicating the bridleway. Pass through two small gates and then descend the hill to the gate beside the terraced house.

[9] Turn right and continue along the road ignoring the first bridleway on the left, a short distance later there is a small stony lay-by, take the right of the two bridleways alongside the river.

[10] On reaching the road turn left, continue straight ahead at the cross-roads past the Old School House. At the junction with the main road turn right past the White Horse Inn. After approximately 200 metres take the bridleway on the right to Durweston, follow this under the railway arch over the river and past the mill house to the road.

[11] Turn left and then right at Durweston Cross towards Bryanston, continue straight ahead up the hill along the single track road. Once you have reached the top enjoy catching your breath as you speedily descend, turn left at the junction and continue past the farm complex.

[12] At Bryanston Black Fern junction turn right along the no through road. Turn right and then follow the bridleway through the forest. Eventually you will reach open fields, follow the bridleway along the edge before passing through a gate marked 'Keep Shut', continue straight ahead. Follow the main track through the wood eventually reaching open fields once again, follow the bridleway alongside the edge of the fields onto a stony track. Turn left to the road and return to the car park.

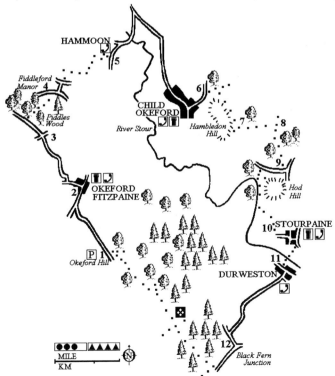

21. Bulbarrow Hill   19/3 miles

START LOCATION AND ACCESS: Bulbarrow Hill is approximately 3 miles from Milton Abbas and is very well sign posted in the locality.
OS MAP REF.: 784059

WARNINGS AND HIGHLIGHTS

♦ Extremely fast descent from Rawlsbury Camp when there is no stock grazing
♦ Potentially fast descent into Winterborne Stickland and towards Ibberton although the second demands greater caution because of the twisty nature of the road and the possibility of meeting a car approaching from the opposite direction
♦ Very, very gruelling climb from Woolland

PUBS

The Fox Inn	Ansty	0258 880328
The Hambro Arms	Milton Abbas	0258 880233
The Shire Horse	Winterborne Stickland	0258 880838
The Crown Inn	Ibberton	0258 817448

PLACES OF INTEREST

Bulbarrow Hill: the second highest point in Dorset offers superb views over the Blackmore Vale, a stone in the car park provides guidance to the various landmarks.
Rawlsbury Camp: a small fortified abode of the hairy iron folk with fantastic views.
Melcombe Bingham and Ansty: the two villages run into one another and if you should be tempted by the very strong ale on offer in the Fox you are likely to do something similar. Nearby Bingham Melcombe house is not open to the public but can be seen from near the 14th century church.
Milton Abbas: see the Winterborne North route.

LINK INFORMATION

The route can be combined with the Winterborne North ride as they both pass through Milton Abbas or alternatively with the Hambledon Hill route at Okeford Hill.

[1] From the Bulbarrow Hill car park take the right fork towards Hazelbury Bryan. After a short distance Rawlsbury Camp will appear on your left, pass through the small entrance gate and follow the bridleway around the edge of the fort. Pass through a small gate and follow the bridleway down the steep hill to a gate between two ponds, go through these gates and continue along the rough road via the farm yard.

[2] At the T junction turn right and then left at the next junction towards Melcombe Bingham. At Ansty Chapel turn right and follow the road past the famous Fox Inn.

[3] At Cross Lanes cross-roads turn left towards Bingham Melcombe House, continue past the House entrance and take the next left. Cross the small ford and turn left.

[4] A short distance before the sharp bend entering the pretty hamlet of Aller take the bridleway on the right along the edge of the field. At the top of the hill turn left on to the road.

[5] Take the first right and descend into the village of Hilton, continue along the road eventually passing Milton Abbey and the school playing fields.

[6] At the junction turn left and climb through the village of Milton Abbas past the Hambro Arms. At the top of the hill turn left and continue past the farm museum and follow the road into Winterborne Stickland.

[7] At the T junction turn left and continue past the Shire Horse and then on through the next village, Turnworth.

[8] At the top of the hill immediately before Okeford Hill picnic site car park take the sign posted bridleway on the left.

[9] On reaching the road turn left and then right towards Ibberton. The descent is very steep and has several sharp bends. At the T junction turn left (if you wish to visit the attractive village of Ibberton turn right and then retrace your route).

[10] At Woolland junction turn left to Bulbarrow, at the top of the climb look for an oxygen tent and then turn left and follow the road back to the car park. The route can be shortened in a number of places by simply following the signs to Bulbarrow.

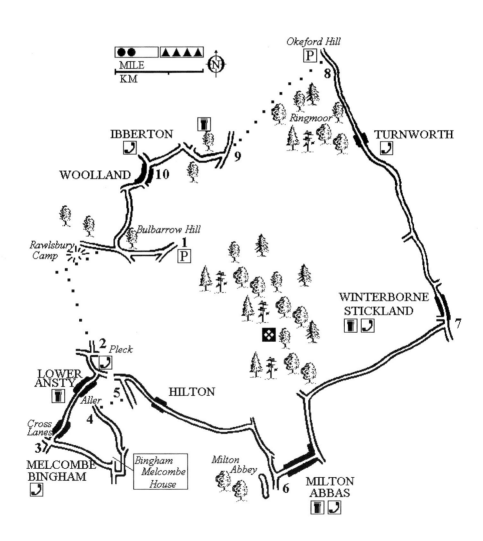

Six of the best . . .
off-road descents

The following descents are all potentially very fast and also dangerous. I am not recommending them so anyone can cycle recklessly but merely to point out they exist for those who enjoy the thrill of a bumpy descent.

Nine Barrow down to Ulwell (3)
Very bumpy fast track with a gate halfway down

Peters Gore junction through Gypsies End (10)
Very fast and bumpy track

Swyre Head towards Kimmeridge (2)
Another potentially very fast but deeply rutted track

Rawlesbury Camp towards Pleck (21)
Very steep descent through grassy meadow. Take care if stock are grazing

The descent near Culpeppers Dish (6)
So steep it is almost not possible to ride and a mistake might be the quickest way of entering the Vienna boys' choir

Descent into Winterborne Abbas (8)
Very, very bumpy rutted track.

Six of the best . . .
off-road climbs

Ulwell to Nine Barrow (3)
Long drag along a bumpy track that gets steeper the further you climb

Ascent to Ridgeway Hill from near Church Knowle (2)
Extremely steep climb on grassy track thankfully not that long

Lower Rew towards the Hardy Monument (8)
Long drag along stony track

Corfe Castle to Renscombe Hill (2)
Long climb that gets steeper near the top along chalky track

Bridleway beyond Littlebredy towards Kingston Russell (8)
Short sharp climb on bumpy track

Plush towards Alton Pancras (22)
Very, very demanding if the track is wet

22. Piddle Valley   15/7 miles

START LOCATION AND ACCESS: Piddlehinton lies on the B3143 and is well sign posted from Dorchester.
OS MAP REF.: 716972
NEAREST RAILWAY STATION: Maiden Newton or Dorchester

WARNINGS AND HIGHLIGHTS
♦ Some of the bridleways are very muddy even in the summer
♦ Potentially very dangerous descent to Folly Farm
♦ Extremely testing climb out of Plush, especially if it is wet
♦ Exciting fast bumpy descent into Alton Pancras
♦ Very fast drop into Cerne Abbas and consequently demanding climb out
♦ In places the bridleways are not easy to follow and it is recommended that you carry an OS map
♦ Too many tempting pubs!

PUBS
The Brace of Pheasants	Plush	03004 357
The Royal Oak	Cerne Abbas	0300 341797
The New Inn	Cerne Abbas	0300 341274
The Red Lion	Cerne Abbas	0300 341441
The European Inn	Piddletrenthide	03004 308
The Poachers Inn	Piddletrenthide	03004 358
The Thimble Inn	Piddlehinton	03004 270

PLACES OF INTEREST
Cerne Abbas is a very interesting village where there is much to explore although it is now probably more famous for the largest member of the local community who resides on a nearby hill - the Cerne Giant.

Look out for the unusual pub sign of the Brace of Pheasants.

LINK INFORMATION
To join Sydling Water route follow the road through Cerne Abbas and continue straight ahead at the cross-roads. After approximately one mile take the bridleway on the left past Higher City Farm (3). In addition the ride can also be combined with the Devil's Brook circuit see instruction (3) of that route.

[1] Start at the memorial cross in Piddlehinton. Take the no through road "London Row". Shortly after passing the farm complex on the right the metalled surface ends; continue straight ahead on the stony farm track.

[2] At the bridleway cross-roads continue straight ahead following the deeply rutted muddy lane around the edge of the small wood. Keep straight ahead ignoring the bridleways to the right, at the end of the wood continue straight ahead on the better drained and more easily ridden track. After a short distance, in a more open field you will see a tiny stream on the right, cross this by the small level concrete bridge. Climb the hill along the track between the hedges.

[3] At the road take the bridleway directly opposite to Nettlecombe Farm. Follow the track through the farmyard. After passing through the farm gate follow the bridleway straight ahead along the right-hand edge of the field.

[4] After approximately 1½ miles you will reach a water tank where the bridleway is less defined and more difficult to follow. Proceed to the left roughly in line with the overhead telegraph wires until you reach a thicket in the hedge.

[5] Pass through the wooden gate and make the very tricky descent down the slightly overgrown and bumpy bridleway, on reaching the rutted farm track turn right.

[6] At Folly Farm House turn left and follow the road into Plush.

[7] Shortly after the Brace of Pheasants take the slightly obscured track on the right to Alton Pancras. At the summit of the short but severely testing climb pass through the gate. Turn left and cycle up the hill diagonally away from the hedge to another gate that is just out of sight over the brow of the hill. Pass through the gate onto the stony track, pass through the second gate and then take the right fork down the fast but bumpy and stony track to Alton Pancras.

[8] At the road turn left and follow this for about 250 metres before taking the track on the right. Climb the long drag and then continue straight on past the old barns on your left. Pass through a set of double gates that may be slightly overgrown and then follow the bridleway along the edge of the field to the road.

[9] Turn right and then left down the steep hill into Cerne Abbas. Leave the village on the Piddle Lane to Piddletrenthide. Go straight ahead at the cross-roads. At the next T junction turn right and follow the road along the valley bottom past the three pubs to the start.

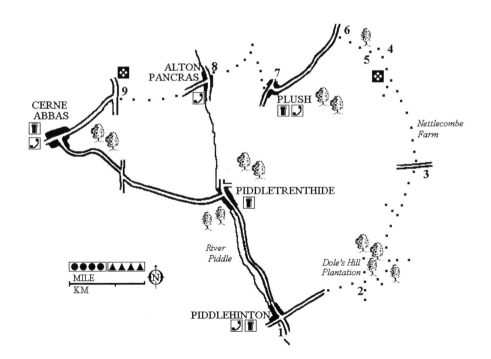

23. The Devil's Brook   11/6 miles

START LOCATION AND ACCESS: Puddletown is on the main road between Poole and Dorchester, the A35.
OS MAP REF.: 756944
NEAREST RAILWAY STATION: Dorchester

WARNINGS AND HIGHLIGHTS
♦ The off road surfaces can be very muddy especially near Dole's Hill Plantation
♦ The Ridge Way is popular with dogs and their owners
♦ Steep climb towards Dewlish

PUBS
The Prince of Wales	Puddletown	0305 848222
The Blue Vinny	Puddletown	0305 848228
The Royal Oak	Dewlish	025 887 352

PLACES OF INTEREST
Dewlish is a pleasant tranquil village.
Puddletown is described on the Puddletown Forest route.

LINK INFORMATION
The ride combines well with the Puddletown Forest ride as they both pass through Puddletown itself. It can also be combined with the Piddle Valley route as the bridleway cross-roads at Dole's Hill Plantation (3) is the one referred to in instruction (2) of that ride.

[1] Start in the centre of Puddletown and follow the main road towards Dorchester. A short distance after the traffic lights take the bridleway on the right that runs past a large white building and continue straight ahead along the wide well used track.

[2] After approximately 2 miles you will reach a road, turn right and speed down the hill. Shortly after passing the Zig Zag sign take the marked bridleway on the right.

[3] After approximately $1\frac{1}{2}$ miles there is a bridleway cross-roads near a small plantation, turn right. The track is very shaded and the surface is more often than not like porridge. Ignore the small track on the left and the marked bridleway on the right. After a short distance the track broadens to a very small clearing, take the unmarked bridleway on the right and follow this straight ahead alongside the hedge.

[4] On reaching the road turn left and then right to Dewlish.

[5] At the cross-roads in the village turn right towards Puddletown. At the Blue Vinny Inn turn left and follow the road back into Puddletown.

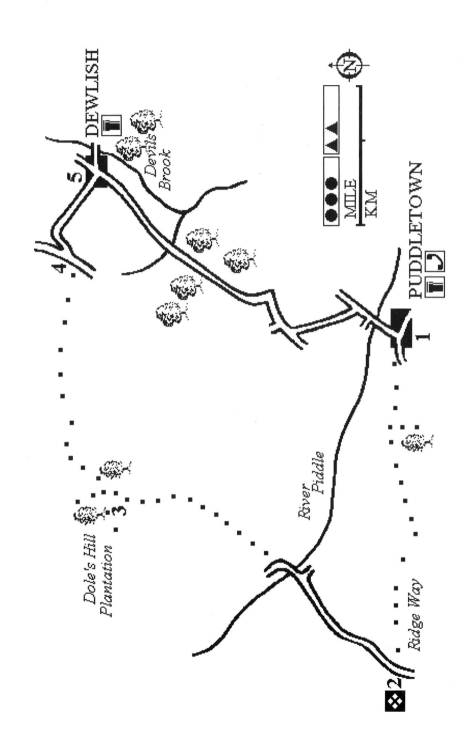

DEWLISH

Devils Brook

Dole's Hill Plantation

River Piddle

Ridge Way

PUDDLETOWN

N

MILE
KM

1
2
3
4
5

63

24.   The Winterbornes (N)   17/9 miles

START LOCATION AND ACCESS: Winterborne Kingston is on the road that links the A35(T) and the A354 and is well sign posted.
OS MAP REF.: 862977
NEAREST RAILWAY STATION: Wool

WARNINGS AND HIGHLIGHTS
♦ Fast bumpy descent towards Winterborne Clenston
♦ Fast stony descent to the A354
♦ Fast descent along rutted track towards Anderson
♦ Several stiff climbs that are especially testing when the conditions are muddy

PUBS
The Greyhound Inn	Winterborne Kingston	0929 471332
The Hambro Arms	Milton Abbas	0258 880233

PLACES OF INTEREST
Milton Abbas: beautiful 'model' village, the impressive Abbey and school, St. Catherines Chapel and the nearby Park Farm Museum makes it worth spending some time in this delightful spot. 0258 880216

Look out for an interesting thatched round barn before Winterborne Whitechurch, the manor house and pretty church (just south of the village) in Winterborne Clenston and towards the end of the route Anderson Manor and the peculiar crop in a field on the right approaching Winterborne Kingston.

LINK INFORMATION
To join the Winterbornes south ride follow route directions from the T junction at the end of the road from Anderson.
The route can also be connected to the Bulbarrow route in Milton Abbas.

[1] From the centre of Winterborne Kingston follow the road to Winterborne Whitechurch, on reaching the cross-roads continue straight ahead to Milton Abbas.

[2] Once in Milton Abbas turn right along the Forestry Commission private road past the entrance to the Milton Manor Hotel. Follow the stony track into the forest until you reach a gate/barrier across the route; take the marked bridleway on the left up the steep incline. The bridleways through the forest are quite well marked and fairly easy to follow. On reaching another forest track turn left and then take the marked bridleway on the right that climbs through the trees to rejoin the stony track. Turn right and proceed straight along this. Pass straight through the cross-roads after a short distance at the top of the incline you will reach a bridleway fork, take the right prong along the slightly overgrown and potentially very muddy bridleway. Pass through the small gate and follow the well-defined track down the edge of the field to the road; turn right.

[3] Shortly after the manor house take the bridleway on the left towards Blandford St. Mary. You will eventually reach a small gate pass through it and the jungle beyond it into an open field. Turn left and trace the bridleway along the edge of the field. At the next gate turn right and follow the well-used farm access track down the hill. On reaching the T junction at the base of the hill turn right past the farm buildings to the road; turn right.

[4] Take the next road on the left and then turn right along the no through road. Near the top of the hill, when the metalled road curves to the left, continue straight ahead on the stony track. At the foot of the hill pass through the gate and then follow the bridleway to the right up the hill beside the hedge.

[5] At the top of the hill pass through the gate and cycle around to the left for a few metres before taking the first bridleway on the right. Continue on the track as it curves to the left around the edge of the wood past the observation tower built into a tree. Pass through the gateposts in the hedge and proceed straight across the field before the bridleway joins a stony track. Follow this track and at the bottom of the hill you will pass Anderson Manor and a farm yard before reaching the road. Turn right and return to Winterborne Kingston.

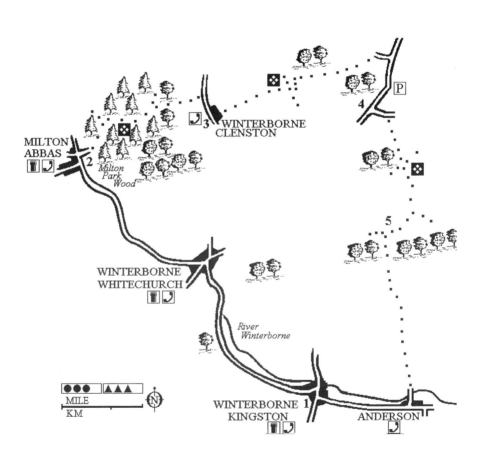

25. The Winterbornes (S) 12/5 miles

START LOCATION AND ACCESS: Bere Regis is well sign posted from the A31(T) and the A35. The location of the car park is well marked in the village.
OS MAP REF.: 846947
NEAREST RAILWAY STATION: Wool

WARNINGS AND HIGHLIGHTS
♦ The bridleway beyond Warren House tends to be overgrown in the summer
♦ Fast stony tracks through the forest
♦ Walkers and dogs
♦ Muddy track away from Winterborne Kingston
♦ Fast bumpy decent down a rutted track to the Bere Regis by-pass with short braking distance

PUBS
The Royal Oak	Bere Regis	0929 471203
The Drax Arms	Bere Regis	0929 471386
The Greyhound Inn	Winterborne Kingston	0929 471332

PLACES OF INTEREST
Bere Regis: quiet village that has benefitted from it's by-pass. The attractive church of St. John the Baptist is well worth visiting to see the roof.

LINK INFORMATION
To join the Wareham Forest ride take the gravel track on the right before Bere Lodge. Return to the original route by turning right at the junction in Bloxworth.
To join the Winterbornes North ride turn right at the T junction in Winterborne Kingston and then left to Winterborne Whitechurch.

[1] From the car park in Bere Regis turn left, left again and then right at the T junction.

[2] After 2 miles you will cross a small bridge, after a short distance turn left along a stony track that initially runs parallel to some electricity pylons. Continue along the track passing Warren House before entering the wood. Cycle through the woods on the way crossing a small stream, pass by the paddocks and then through the timber yard to the road; turn left.

[3] When the road curves sharply to the left, almost at right angles, continue straight ahead along the gravel track past Bere Lodge into the forest. The bridleway through the forest is well marked and easy to follow. On reaching the road cross it with care and continue straight ahead on the gravel track until it veers to the right. Go straight on along the less obvious sand and grass track indicated by the bridleway marker.

[4] Cross the busy road with care taking the road directly opposite to Bloxworth. At the T junction near the thatched shelter turn left and then follow the road round to the right.

[5] At the T junction turn left.

[6] At Red Post junction continue straight ahead to Anderson, continue through the village to Winterborne Kingston.

[7] At the T junction take the track directly opposite, keep straight ahead until you reach a bridleway cross-roads almost surrounded by gates, turn left up the slight incline on the chalky track. At the end keep straight ahead onto the grassy lane ignoring the more obvious track to the left.

[8] Cross the busy by-pass onto the track opposite and follow this into the village. At the T junction turn left and then follow the signs back to the car park.

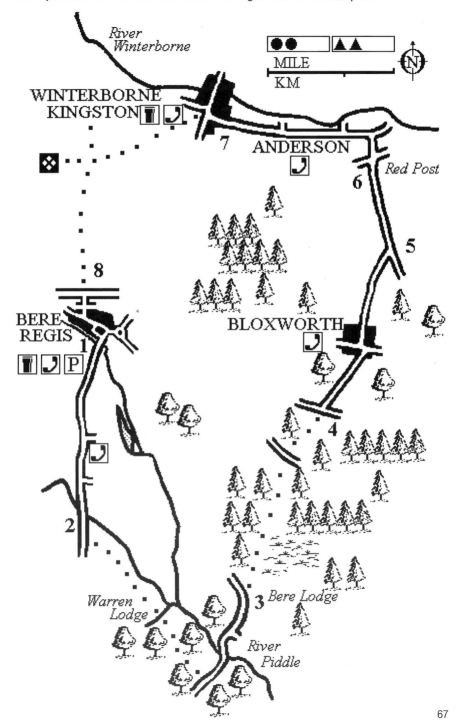

26. Wareham Forest   16/7 miles

START LOCATION AND ACCESS: Sherford Bridge is on the B3075 the road linking the A35 and the A351.
OS MAP REF.: 919927
NEAREST RAILWAY STATION: Wareham

WARNINGS AND HIGHLIGHTS
♦ Very muddy conditions (a quagmire) to be expected between Sherford Bridge and Organford. In really bad weather it would be easier to cycle on porridge.
♦ Fast gravel tracks through the forest
♦ Walkers and dogs

PUBS

The Rose & Crown	Lytchett Matravers	0202 625325
The Chequers	Lytchett Matravers	0202 622215
The Cock & Bottle	Morden	092 945 238

Look out for the large Charborough Park estate and the very attractive cottage near Morden Drove.

LINK INFORMATION
To join the Winterborne South ride turn right after the thatched shelter in Bloxworth rather than left. To re-join the forest ride take the bridleway on the right before Bere Lodge.
The circuit can also be combined with the Roman Road route (see that ride for instructions, page 70).

[1] Start at Sherford Bridge and follow the blue arrows into the forest along the gravel track. Continue straight ahead when the bridleway leaves the forest track.

[2] At the end of the track turn left to the road. Cycle over the bridge and continue straight on.

[3] At the junction with the busy main road turn left and then right towards Lytchett Matravers.

[4] Turn left at the Rose and Crown junction and continue through the village.

[5] After cycling alongside the wall of Charborough Park turn left at Morden Drove junction and follow the road to Morden.

[6] In the village take the left fork at the war memorial.

[7] At the T junction turn right past The Cock and Bottle and then the next left, following the road to Bloxworth.

[8] In Bloxworth turn left at the junction opposite the thatched shelter.

[9] At the next T junction carefully cross the road onto the bridleway directly opposite. Once through the woods cross the road and continue along the bridleway through the forest.

[10] On reaching the road turn left and then almost immediately left again along the gravel bridleway. At the bridleway cross-roads turn left. At the road turn left and then immediately right into the forest car park.

[11] Follow the well-marked bridleway through the forest past Morden Bog and return to Sherford Bridge.

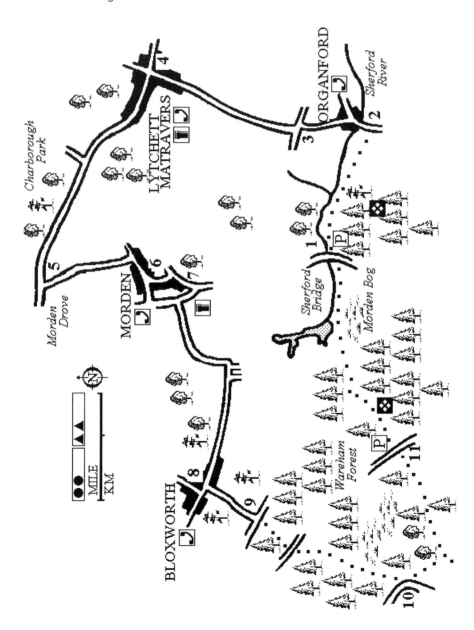

27. The Roman Road   13/3 miles

START LOCATION AND ACCESS: Upton Country Park is on the outskirts of Poole and is well sign posted from the A35.
OS MAP REF.: 992933
NEAREST RAILWAY STATION: Poole or Hamworthy

WARNINGS AND HIGHLIGHTS
◆ The Roman road is a favourite place for dogs to walk their people
◆ Tricky bumpy descent beside Corfe Hills School playing fields
◆ Bridleway to Combe Almer tends to be muddy
◆ Stiff climb into Lytchett Matravers

PUBS
The Chequers	Lytchett Matravers	0202 622215
The Rose and Crown	Lytchett Matravers	0202 625325
The Upton Hotel	Upton	0202 631726

PLACES OF INTEREST
Upton House and Country Park: 19th century house set in 100 acres of beautiful parklands on the edge of Poole Harbour. 0202 672625

Look out for the attractive medieval church in Lytchett Matravers.

LINK INFORMATION
To connect this route to the Wareham Forest circuit turn right rather than left at instruction (10) and follow the road to the Morden Drove junction. In order to return to this route turn right at the Rose and Crown junction once you return to Lytchett Matravers. The route may also be linked with the Trailway route as they both follow the Roman Road for a short stretch.

[1] Start from the Upton Country Park car park and turn left then right at the next two T junctions. Take the first exit on the roundabout to Creekmoor. Take the track on the left between the two logs, after approximately 100 metres continue straight on along the Roman Road.

[2] When you reach the road turn left, from here the Roman Road continues straight ahead on a mixture of made up and unmade up roads and bridleways. Shortly after passing the school playing fields cross the road and take the bridleway slightly to the left. After the stile take the right fork and then follow the sign to Happy Bottom.

[3] On reaching the road turn left and then left again towards Wareham. At the roundabout take the last exit.

[4] At the junction next to Lockyers School turn right and then left down Pardys Hill.

[5] At the foot of the hill turn right along the lane towards Knoll Farm Christian Centre. Continue along the marked bridleway up the tricky incline and then on past Castle Court School.

[6] At the road turn right passing beneath the footbridge, take the next left and then left again.

[7] At the next T junction turn left and then almost immediately right (take the utmost care as many drivers don't along this fast stretch of road). At the next cross-roads turn right towards Sturminster Marshall.

[8] Take the bridleway on the left towards Combe Almer and Duller Lane, the trail is fairly straightforward to follow but in places slightly overgrown before it enters an open field. Continue down the edge of the field passing through a couple of gates before you reach a collection of farm buildings; turn left along the bumpy track between the hedges.

[9] At the road turn left.

[10] At the next T junction turn left; climb the hill past the church into Lytchett Matravers and then on past the Chequers and the Rose and Crown out of the village.

[11] At the T junction just beyond the Courtyard Craft Centre turn right and then left over the flyover to Upton. At the complicated roundabout system near The Upton Hotel continue straight ahead past the parade of shops to return to the Country Park.

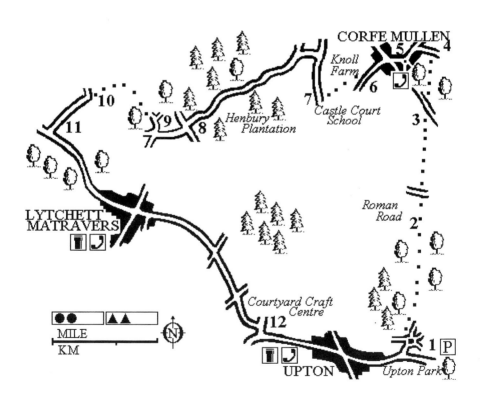

28. Badbury Rings

19/7 miles

START LOCATION AND ACCESS: Badbury Rings is well sign posted on the main
Wimborne - Blandford road, the B3082
OS MAP REF.: 972032
NEAREST RAILWAY STATION: Poole

WARNINGS AND HIGHLIGHTS
♦ Parts of the route seem to provide the ideal conditions for the cultivation of stinging
  nettles
♦ Tricky bridleway through Holly Grove
♦ Some of the bridleways are infrequently used

PUBS
The Drovers Inn	Gussage All Saints	0258 840084
The Stocks Inn	Furzehill	0202 88248

PLACES OF INTEREST
Badbury Rings: one of the many superb hill forts now owned by the National Trust.
Lodge Farm: medieval hunting lodge. 0202 880575

LINK INFORMATION
To add the Gussage route (8) continue straight ahead on the bridleway to Harley
Down, re-join the route in the village of Gussage All Saints. As the ride has the same
start location as the Tarrant Valley and Shapwick routes it is very easy to combine
them.

[1] From the Badbury Rings car park follow the marked bridleway from the road
towards the large hedge. Pass around the gate and climb the hill, follow the
bridleway straight ahead through the wood until you reach a gravel track; turn left
down the hill.

[2] As the track levels off and curves to the right continue straight ahead along the
grassy bridleway between the hedges until you reach a road. Turn left.

[3] Go straight ahead at the cross-roads and follow the road to Manswood.

[4] Turn right towards Witchampton past the bus shelter. Take the bridleway on the
left to Half Moon and Cock Road, when the track forks take the right route and on
reaching the road follow it straight ahead past Cockroad Farm.

[5] Take the bridleway on the left, after a short distance follow the sign to the right and
continue down the tricky root strewn track on through the ford to the road.

[6] Take the bridleway almost directly opposite to the Ringwood - Shaftesbury road.

[7] On reaching the road cross it very carefully - people seem to be in a hurry to get to
Shaftesbury and Ringwood. Take the bridleway to Holly Grove; the narrow track
twists and turns through the copse and is steep in places.

[8] At the road turn right and follow it into Gussage All Saints, continue past The
Drovers Inn to Amen Corner junction, turn right.

[9] At the T junction turn left and then right to Moor Crichel and Witchampton follow
the road past the Crichel Estate.

[10] Turn left at the juction with a tree surrounded by a wooden seat.

[11] At the T junction turn right through the village of Witchampton following the sign posted route towards Wimborne.

[12] Go straight ahead at the cross-roads towards Gaunts Common and Holt.

[13] At the T junction turn right towards Furzehill.

[14] At Pig Oak junction turn right. Turn right immediately after the Stocks Inn.

[15] Go straight ahead at the cross-roads to High Hall and Barnsley, yes indeed Barnsley.

[16] At the end of the metalled surface take the second track on the left (the one that is almost at right angles). Follow the stony track past the black barn, at the bridleway cross-roads turn right and continue along the stony track. At the next bridleway cross-roads continue straight ahead. You will reach a small wood at the top of the hill and the track you followed at the beginning of the ride, turn left and retrace your route back to the start.

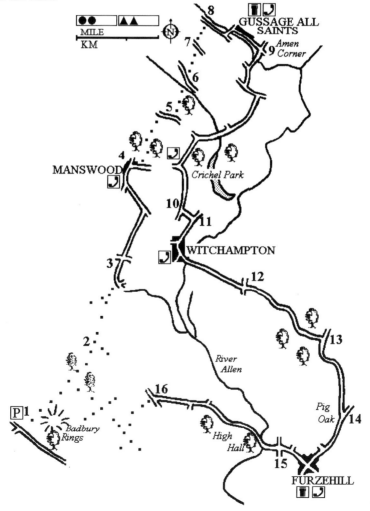

29. Shapwick

START LOCATION AND ACCESS: Badbury Rings is well sign posted on the main Wimborne - Blandford road, the B3082.
OS MAP REF.: 972032
NEAREST RAILWAY STATION: Poole

WARNINGS AND HIGHLIGHTS
♦ Peaceful lanes that are popular with dogs and their owners
♦ Fast descent from the Vine Inn down narrow road with short stopping distance

PUBS
The Vine Inn	Pamphill	0202 882259
The Anchor Inn	Shapwick	0258 857269

PLACES OF INTEREST
Badbury Rings: one of the many superb hill forts now owned by the National Trust.
Lodge Farm: medieval hunting lodge. 0202 880575
Kingston Lacy: magnificent house and park land owned by the National Trust. 0202 883402
The Court House at Cowgrove: a very worthwhile and painstaking renovation by the NT.

LINK INFORMATION
This route can easily be combined with the Badbury Rings ride as they both have the same start location or alternatively with the Tarrant Valley route simply by continuing along the road from Shapwick until you reach the memorial cross and then take the bridleway on the right.

[1] Leave the car park on the access road and then turn left and follow the bridleway that runs parallel to the road beside the trees.

[2] At Lodge Farm cross the busy road and move to the right in order to take the marked bridleway on the left. Follow the bridleway straight ahead until you reach the road, turn left.

[3] At St. Stephen's church turn right along the avenue of trees beside the cricket pitch and on past the Vine Inn. At the base of the hill turn right and continue past the Court House at Cowgrove.

[4] At the T junction turn right and then take the road to Shapwick. Follow the road past the Anchor Inn through the village continuing past Bishop's Court Farm before taking the marked bridleway on the right just beyond the village sign. Shortly after passing the cream cottage turn left along the bridleway known as Swan Lane to the Badbury Avenue. On reaching the road turn right and follow the road back to Badbury Rings.

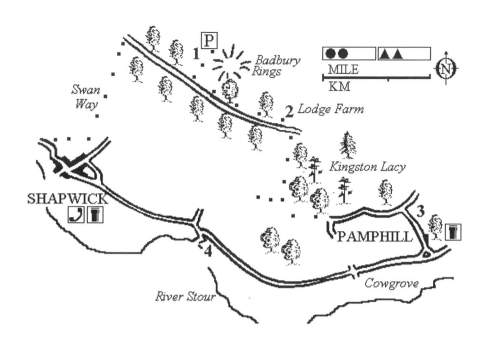

Swan Way

SHAPWICK

Badbury Rings

Lodge Farm

Kingston Lacy

PAMPHILL

Cowgrove

River Stour

MILE
KM

The Vine Inn

30. The Tarrant Valley   18/13 miles

START LOCATION AND ACCESS: Badbury Rings is well sign posted on the main Wimborne - Blandford road the B3082.
OS MAP REF.: 972032
NEAREST RAILWAY STATION: Poole

WARNINGS AND HIGHLIGHTS
♦ A lot of the offroad riding is on well maintained farm access tracks
♦ Rough bumpy bridleway from Buzbury Rings to Lophill Farm
♦ Avoid Lophill Farm during milking times
♦ Very quiet especially when you consider the good quality riding and the close proximity to the large urban conurbation

PUBS
Unfortunately I have made a mistake on this ride as the route fails to pass a pub, I just can't understand how it happened.

PLACES OF INTEREST
Badbury Rings. Lookout for the Buzbury Rings near Ashley Wood golfcourse.

LINK INFORMATION
As this route has the same start location as the Badbury Rings and Shapwick rides it is easy to combine them at various points on the route.
To make the route a true exploration of the Tarrant Valley the ride can be connected to the Pimperne circuit by turning left instead of right at the end of direction (6). Follow the road through the beautiful village of Tarrant Monkton, and then Tarrant Launceston. Cross the busy A354 and proceed through Tarrant Hinton. Join the Pimperne route at the junction near the entrance to White Kennels, look out for the small post box, just before entering Tarrant Gunville. Return by the same route.

[1] Start in the Badbury Rings car park and follow the marked bridleway away from the road towards the gate in the woody hedge. Pass around the gate and climb the hill, continuing through the woods until you reach a gravel track; turn left down the hill.

[2] As the track levels off and curves to the right go straight ahead along the grassy bridleway between the hedges; follow this until you reach a road. Turn left.

[3] Continue straight ahead at the cross-roads towards Manswood. Take the marked bridleway on the left between the large logs, and follow the well-worn track until it reaches the road.

[4] Proceed straight ahead on the road for a short distance and then turn left along the bridleway towards Common Drove and the A354. Follow the well-marked bridleway along the stony track eventually reaching a complicated track junction known as Six Ways. Counting in a clockwise direction take the third exit, almost straight on, (the bridleway direction is indicated on a small plaque attached to a wooden post). Continue on the main stony track as it meanders through the wood.

[5] Once through the wood turn right at the next T junction and then left at the cross-roads at the foot of the hill.

[6] At the T junction beside the reservoir turn left and continue past the barrier straight on ignoring the track to the right, at the next T junction turn right. Near the end of the wood follow the track around to the left onto the metalled surface until you reach the road junction; turn right and then left at the base of the steep hill towards Tarrants Rushton and Keyneston.

[7] After cycling along the road for approximately 1 mile take the bridleway on the right to Buzbury Rings, the route is well used and is clearly marked. Eventually you will reach an area of metalled track just before Ashley Wood golfcourse; ignore the gates and follow the track around to the left alongside the wood. On reaching the road turn right.

[8] Shortly after Buzbury Rings take the grassy bridleway on the right to Charlton Marshall. Although the bridleway does not appear to be frequently used it is clearly marked with blue arrows and is on the whole easy to follow. At the end of the lane pass through the gate and proceed straight ahead along the right-hand edge of the field to another gate. Pass through the gate and follow the bridleway along the left hand edge of the fields eventually passing through Lophill Farm yard to the road; turn left.

[9] Cycle along the road for approximately $1\frac{1}{4}$ miles before reaching a small junction with a memorial cross; turn left and then take the marked bridleway straight ahead.

[10] When you reach the road cross it with care in order to join the bridleway to Witchampton. At the end of the slightly overgrown grassy lane turn right onto the concrete track. Take care to follow the blue arrows as after some distance the bridleway leaves the stony track and follows a more grassy route across the field to a fork, take the right prong. Turn right at the T junction to retrace your earlier tyre tracks back to the car park at Badbury Rings.

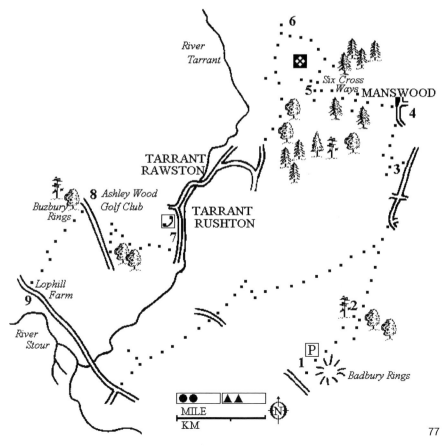

31. The Trailway   12/8 miles

START LOCATION AND ACCESS: Broadstone is on the outskirts of Poole towards Wimborne and is well sign posted from both towns
OS MAP REF.: 004959

WARNINGS AND HIGHLIGHTS
- The Trailway is very popular and well used by walkers and cyclists alike
- The whole route definitely passes through horse country, there are many stables and many riders
- Upton Heath is an SSSI
- Some of Stony Down Plantation is very muddy
- There are several blind corners on the quiet roads

PUBS
The Holme Bush	Beacon Hill	0202 659420
The Lambs Green Inn	Corfe Mullen	0202 889191
The Willett Arms	Merley	0202 883144

PLACES OF INTEREST
Broadstone and Corfe Mullen are expanding villages on the edge of Poole that still retain some of their old world charm, and although this route does not have any tourist attractions it feels like you are deep in the country for much of the ride whilst you are never more than five miles from the centre of Poole. The local council should be commended for their foresight in converting the old railway into the Trailway and I hope this scheme can be expanded further. There are many attractive cottages and beautiful views along the route lookout for the nature reserve at Delph Woods.
A nearby attraction is the Merley Bird Garden (0202 883790).

LINK INFORMATION: The route can easily be linked with the Roman Road ride as they both follow the same bridleway for a short distance.

[1] Head away from the Broadstone Sport Centre follow the path under the sub way to join the Trailway on the opposite side of the busy road. Follow the track straight ahead, after approximately $1\frac{1}{2}$ miles the track passes over the old railway bridge just before you reach this veer off to the left down the steep slope. Pass through the stile and turn right following the track towards Corfe Mullen.

[2] When you reach the road turn left and then take the first left, Beacon Road follow this right to it's unmade up end on the edge of Upton Heath. The bridleway dog legs roughly to the right across the heath but is not very well marked. There are many tracks, I have tried to describe the route as I see it but as there are so many alternatives, my general advice would be to generally veer to the right. Whatever you do don't let this garbled nonsense put you off as there is some excellent riding. Follow the track straight ahead and then veer to the right down a steep gully, at the bottom continue on the track towards the right. Cross the cutting the stream has eroded and follow the track beside this up the steep incline. At the top of the climb follow the track to the left towards an area fenced off with angled concrete posts. When you almost reach the fence follow the track to the right (in the direction of the man made mound with the just visible trig point on top) for a few metres before taking the track on the left heading towards the road in the distance. The track like so many on the heath is very bumpy and rutted as the area is well used by horses and although this makes some of the riding difficult it is far from impossible. Near the aforementioned mound there are a couple of picnic tables and an area that appears to be popular with cyclists wishing to whiz over bumps and humps and take "air".

[3] At the road turn left, just before the Holme Bush Inn take the marked bridleway on the right. At the end of the track turn right and follow the road for a few hundred metres before taking the marked bridleway on the left just before an area used as a small lay-by. Follow the bridleway through the plantation it is well marked and easy to follow despite the fact that if frequently does not follow the main forest tracks.

[4] Once through the woods follow the road straight ahead and before taking the first turning on the right. Turn right at the next T junction. Shortly after passing beneath the footbridge take the marked bridleway on the left to Pardys Hill, continue past the school. At the end of the track pass by the gate onto the narrow and bumpy track, turn right at the metalled surface. When you reach the road turn left and then take the next left, Sleight Lane.

[5] At the top of the hill continue straight ahead at the offset cross-roads, take care as you are crossing slightly blind and cars tend to accelerate into this bend. Follow the road straight ahead. Shortly after passing beneath the disused railway bridge there is a junction at which you should give way although the road appears to go straight ahead so take care.

[6] At the cross-roads continue straight ahead past the Lambs Green Inn. Turn right at the next T junction. At the end of the road pass through the gate onto the bridleway marked B.R. 114 turn right after passing beneath the flyover and follow the track to its end.

[7] When you reach the road turn right over the flyover and continue past the Willett Arms after a short distance there is an entrance to a track on the left pass through the stile and follow the Trailway back to Broadstone.

Six of the best . . .
road climbs

Hooke to Rampisham Hill (9)
A very long and gruelling climb to show you what the granny ring is for.

The climb out of Durweston (20)
A long and very arduous ascent along a narrow road with passing (or do I mean resting) places.

The return to Shaftesbury (16)
Undoubtedly one of the most demanding climbs.

Woolland to Bulbarrow (21)
Simply the toughest climb on any of the routes either on the road or off.

The Friary to Batcombe Hill (13)
A very long hill that is extremely steep towards the top.

Abbotsbury to the Hardy Monument (7)
A very long and demanding climb.